The POWER OF WOMEN IN LEADERSHIP

Build Confidence, Achieve Work-Life Balance,
and Advance Your Career Authentically

KARINA G. JAUREGUI

© **Copyright 2025 Karina G. Jauregui - All rights reserved.**

The content within this book may not be reproduced, duplicated, or transmitted without direct written permission from the author or the publisher.

Under no circumstances will any blame or legal responsibility be held against the publisher or author for any damages, reparation, or monetary loss due to the information contained within this book. Either directly or indirectly. You are responsible for your own choices, actions, and results.

This book is copyright-protected. This book is only for personal use. You cannot amend, distribute, sell, use, quote, or paraphrase any part of this book's content without the author's or publisher's consent.

Please note that the information contained within this document is for educational purposes only. All effort has been expended to present accurate, up-to-date, reliable, and complete information. No warranties of any kind are declared or implied. Readers acknowledge that the author does not render legal, financial, medical, or professional advice. The content within this book has been derived from various sources. Please consult a licensed professional before attempting any techniques outlined in this book.

By reading this document, the reader agrees that under no circumstances is the author responsible for any losses, direct or indirect, which are incurred as a result of the use of the information contained within this document, including, but not limited to, — errors, omissions, or inaccuracies.

To the amazing and talented women I am blessed to have in my life:

*Mom, a true example of kindness and courage.
My sisters, always honest, supportive, and willing to help.
And to my daughter, who fills my heart with joy and inspires me to keep growing and be the best example for her.*

*I love you all deeply.
Thank you for standing by me through both the good times and the challenging moments.*

Content

Introduction 9

Chapter 1: Building Unshakeable Confidence 11

    1.1 Understanding the Confidence Gap in Women Leaders 11

    1.2 Identifying and Leveraging Your Unique Strengths 15

    1.3 Embracing Vulnerability as a Confidence Builder 20

    1.4 Overcoming Imposter Syndrome with Cognitive Strategies 22

    1.5 Developing a Growth Mindset for Leadership Success 27

    1.6 Celebrating Small Wins to Build Momentum 31

Chapter 2: Authentic Leadership Styles 35

    2.1 Your Leadership Style 35

    2.2 Leading with Empathy and Emotional Intelligence 41

    2.3 Crafting Your Personal Leadership Brand 47

    2.4 Balancing Assertiveness and Approachability 51

    2.5 Authentic Decision-Making: Aligning Choices with Values 53

    2.6 The Power of Storytelling in Authentic Leadership 57

Chapter 3: Navigating Workplace Dynamics 59

    3.1 Understanding Workplace Politics 59

    3.2 Building Strategic Alliances and Networks 65

    3.3 Communicating with Impact in Male-Dominated Settings 68

    3.4 Leveraging Feedback for Professional Growth 73

    3.5 Handling Criticism and Turning it into Opportunity 78

    3.6 Cultivating a Culture of Collaboration and Inclusion 80

Chapter 4: Mastering Work-Life Balance 83

    4.1 Establishing Boundaries 83

4.2 Delegation: Empowering Your Team and Yourself 86

4.3 Time Management Techniques for Busy Leaders 91

4.4 Creating a Supportive Home Environment 96

4.5 Practicing Mindfulness for Stress Reduction 99

4.6 Self-Care Routines for Sustained Energy 101

Chapter 5: Advancing Your Career Authentically **105**

5.1 Career Roadmap 105

5.2 Navigating Promotions and Negotiations 111

5.3 Building Influence Without Compromise 113

5.4 The Role of Sponsorship in Career Growth 115

5.5 Advocating for Yourself and Others 117

5.6 Leveraging Online Presence for Career Opportunities 120

Chapter 6: Overcoming Systemic Barriers **123**

6.1 Barriers in the Workplace 123

6.2 Strategies for Challenging Gender Bias 128

6.3 Promoting Diversity and Inclusion from Within 130

6.4 Building Allies in Leadership Positions 132

6.5 Leading by Example: Inspiring Systemic Change 134

Chapter 7: Building Strong Networks and Mentorship **137**

7.1 Authentic Networking 137

7.2 Finding and Approaching Potential Mentors 142

7.3 The Mentor-Mentee Relationship: Maximizing Benefits 144

7.4 Sponsorship: Taking Mentorship to the Next Level 146

7.5 Engaging with Professional Communities and Groups 148

7.6 Building a Supportive Network of Peers 153

Chapter 8: Real-World Inspiration and Application **155**

8.1 Trailblazing Women 155
8.2 Case Studies in Authentic Leadership 158
8.3 The Power of Resilience in Leadership Journeys 160
8.4 Your Leadership Legacy: Inspiring Future Generations 162

Conclusion 167

References 171

Introduction

A few years ago, I found myself in a high-stakes boardroom meeting, surrounded by colleagues—mostly men—engaged in a fast-paced, high-pressure discussion. Complex decisions were on the table, and I knew that my insights could add value. Yet, as I prepared to speak, a familiar wave of doubt crept in, a sensation I had learned to recognize over the years. The internal dialogue began almost instinctively: *Would my voice carry weight in this room? Would my perspective be acknowledged, or would it be dismissed, overlooked, or—worse—repeated by someone else and credited to them instead?*

I hesitated for a fraction of a second, long enough to feel the pull of self-doubt but not long enough to surrender to it. Instead, I took a deep breath, straightened my posture, and leaned in—both physically and mentally—into the space I had earned. With clarity and conviction, I spoke. The room fell silent. The side conversations faded. People turned to listen, not out of courtesy, but because what I had to say mattered. At that moment, I felt something shift—not just in the room but within me.

That experience solidified a truth I had always known but had not always embraced: Leadership is not just about expertise or experience; it's about confidence, presence, and the willingness to claim your space at the table. It's about speaking up even when doubt lingers and leading authentically despite the pressures to conform. That day was not the first time I had to navigate these challenges, and it certainly wasn't the last. But it was a defining moment—a reminder of the power we wield when we choose to step into our leadership with courage and conviction.

This book is your guide to building confidence, achieving work-life balance, and advancing your career authentically. It addresses women's unique challenges in leadership, offering strategies and insights to empower you on this journey.

Women in leadership face distinct obstacles. Gender bias remains prevalent, and the struggle to integrate work and life demands is ongoing. Many women contend with a confidence gap, questioning their abilities despite evidence to the contrary. Statistics prove that women underestimate their performance and potential, unlike their male counterparts. These challenges are real, but they are not unbeatable.

Yet, the transformative power of women in leadership is undeniable. Women bring strengths like emotional intelligence, empathy, and collaborative approaches. These qualities foster inclusive environments, drive innovation, and inspire teams to achieve more. Women leaders can redefine leadership paradigms, making organizations stronger and more resilient.

This book is structured to guide you through key areas essential to your leadership journey. We begin by exploring how to build confidence, understanding its foundation, and developing it through actionable strategies. Next, we tackle the perennial issue of achieving work-life balance, providing practical tools for setting boundaries and prioritizing effectively. We then delve into advancing your career authentically, emphasizing the importance of leading with integrity and building influence.

Each chapter includes real-world examples and lessons from successful women leaders. These stories inspire and validate, showing that you are not alone in your challenges and triumphs. The book includes many interactive elements like self-assessments, reflection prompts, and action plans. These tools are designed to make the content actionable and relatable, encouraging you to apply the insights to your journey.

In the following pages, let us explore the power of women in leadership, uncover the strengths and strategies that will propel you forward, and build a community of women who lead boldly and inspire others to do the same. Your journey begins here, and I am honored to be a part of it.

CHAPTER 1: BUILDING UNSHAKEABLE CONFIDENCE

"No one can make you feel inferior without your consent."
— Eleanor Roosevelt

1.1 Understanding the Confidence Gap in Women Leaders

The confidence gap comes from societal expectations and gender biases that have shaped women's roles for years. Historically, leadership has been associated with traits perceived as masculine —decisiveness, assertiveness, and competitiveness. These stereotypes have often marginalized women's leadership styles, which tend to emphasize collaboration, empathy, and emotional intelligence. As a result, women may internalize a belief that they do not fit the traditional mold of a leader, which can erode confidence. The historical lack of female representation in executive roles compounds this challenge. The absence of visible role models in leadership positions has perpetuated the myth that women are less suited for such roles. The scarcity of women in top positions reinforces these stereotypes and limits opportunities for mentorship and support, further widening the confidence gap.

Research consistently underscores this disparity. A notable study from Cornell University reveals that men often overestimate their abilities, while women underestimate theirs, even when their actual performance is comparable [†1]. This phenomenon, known as self-assessment bias, is a significant factor in the confidence gap. Additionally, surveys on leadership ambition levels indicate that women tend to have lower expectations for advancement than their male counterparts. This is not due to a lack of ambition but rather a reflection of the barriers they anticipate. Workplace confidence assessments also show that women's confidence tends to increase with experience and age, suggesting that the gap is not an inherent flaw but a result of external influences [†1]. These insights highlight the need to address the structural and cultural barriers contributing to the confidence gap.

The impact of this gap on career progression is profound. Women often hesitate to pursue leadership roles, negotiate promotions, and pay raises due to self-doubt. The fear of taking on bigger responsibilities comes from self-doubt, not a lack of ability. This hesitation can result in missed opportunities and slower career advancement. Lower negotiation success rates also reflect this phenomenon. Women may enter negotiations less assertively, fearing backlash or being perceived as overly aggressive. This cautious approach often leads to outcomes that do not fully reflect their worth or contributions.

Cultivating self-awareness is imperative to effectively bridge this gap. This journey begins with a critical examination of the internal narratives that chip away at one's self-assurance. Through introspection, women can uncover the personal barriers that stand between them and a robust sense of confidence. Journaling emerges as a potent tool in this endeavor, offering a reflective mirror for one's thoughts, achievements, and goals. This simple yet profound practice can illuminate insights and foster a greater sense of clarity and perspective.

Building confidence is not a process of reinvention but one of authentic self-acceptance and growth. It's about acknowledging and leveraging one's unique strengths to lead with genuine authenticity.

Reflection Exercise:

Identifying Confidence Barriers

Take some time to reflect on your confidence barriers. Follow the prompts provided for each step and fill out the corresponding columns:

Step:	*Reflection Questions:*	*Your Notes:*
Identify Areas of Least Confidence	*What areas of leadership or life do you feel least confident in?*	
Document Situations That Trigger Self-Doubt	*What specific situations or scenarios cause you to feel unsure of yourself?*	
Analyze Contributing Factors	*What societal expectations or personal factors contribute to these feelings?*	

Examine Internalized Narratives	*What negative narratives or beliefs have you internalized about your abilities?*	
Challenge Limiting Beliefs	*Is there evidence to support or disprove these beliefs? Are they valid?*	
Replace Negative Self-Talk	*How can you reframe these beliefs into positive affirmations that emphasize your achievements and potential?*	

1.2 Identifying and Leveraging Your Unique Strengths

As you navigate the complex leadership landscape, understanding your unique strengths becomes a pivotal element of your success. It starts with a thorough assessment of your skills and attributes, an introspective exercise that allows you to pinpoint what sets you apart.

Personality assessments like the *StrengthsFinder* offer a structured approach to uncovering these traits. These tools analyze your responses to various scenarios, revealing patterns and tendencies that highlight your core competencies. These assessments, combined with feedback from peers and mentors, give you a well-rounded view of your strengths. Colleagues and advisors who see you in various situations can provide valuable insights you might not notice on your own. Their perspectives can illuminate strengths you might underestimate or overlook. This dual approach—using both assessments and external feedback—creates a robust framework for identifying your strengths, laying the groundwork for leveraging them effectively.

Once you have identified your strengths, leveraging them becomes the next step in enhancing your leadership effectiveness. Recognizing your unique attributes allows you to tailor your leadership style, aligning it with what comes naturally to you. This alignment fosters authenticity, a key component of effective leadership.

When you lead in a manner that reflects your true self, you inspire trust and confidence in those around you. For example, if you possess a natural aptitude for empathy, integrating this into your leadership approach can create an environment where team members feel valued and understood. By emphasizing your empathetic nature, you can build a culture of openness and collaboration, encouraging innovation and accountability within your team.

To assist in this process, practical tools like the **SWOT** analysis—an acronym for **S**trengths, **W**eaknesses, **O**pportunities, and **T**hreats—can be invaluable. This framework provides a structured method for evaluating how your strengths can be applied to leadership roles and challenges. By understanding your strengths within the context of your environment, you can identify opportunities where you can excel. For instance, a leader with strong organizational skills might thrive in roles requiring meticulous project management. Meanwhile, understanding potential threats or challenges allows you to proactively address areas where your strengths may need reinforcement. These insights empower you to make informed decisions about your career path, aligning your strengths with roles that offer fulfillment and impact.

Aligning your strengths with leadership roles enhances your effectiveness and contributes to greater job satisfaction. When your responsibilities align with your natural abilities, you experience a sense of fulfillment and purpose. This alignment is crucial for sustained motivation and engagement. Consider a scenario where a leader with excellent communication skills finds a role that involves public speaking and stakeholder engagement. Such alignment enables them to perform at their best, leveraging their skills to influence and inspire. Moreover, understanding your strengths can help you build teams that complement your abilities. By surrounding yourself with individuals whose strengths differ from your own, you create a balanced team capable of tackling diverse challenges. This diversity in skills ensures that all aspects of a project are addressed with expertise and precision.

Interactive Element:

Strengths Mapping Exercise

- **Identify Your Core Strengths:**
  List your key leadership strengths.

    1)

    2)

    3)

  Reflect on how these strengths positively impact your current role.

    1)

    2)

    3)

- **Assess Weaknesses:**
  Pinpoint any areas where you feel less confident or capable.

  Consider how these weaknesses might hinder your ability to fully leverage your strengths.

- **Explore Opportunities:**
  Identify opportunities within your current role or organization where your strengths can be maximized.

  Look for new projects, responsibilities, or collaborations that align with your skills.

- **Evaluate Threats:**
  Analyze potential threats that could limit your ability to utilize your strengths effectively (e.g., organizational changes, skill gaps, or external pressures).

- **Formulate an Action Plan:**
  Develop strategies to align your strengths with your leadership responsibilities.

Address weaknesses and mitigate threats by setting specific, actionable goals.

1.

2.

3.

o **Monitor and Adjust:**
Regularly revisit your SWOT analysis to ensure your plan aligns with your goals and evolving responsibilities.

1.3 Embracing Vulnerability as a Confidence Builder

In leadership, vulnerability often carries a stigma and is seen as a weakness rather than a strength. Yet, shifting this perspective can transform the way we lead. Vulnerability, when embraced, becomes a powerful tool for building trust and fostering deep connections within a team. Successful leaders like Brené Brown have famously championed the idea that courage and vulnerability are intertwined. Brown's research shows that acknowledging our imperfections humanizes us and strengthens our relationships. Vulnerability invites authenticity, a quality that resonates deeply with others, creating a foundation of trust essential for effective leadership. This trust allows a leader to engage others genuinely, fostering an environment where team members feel safe to express ideas and innovate without fear of judgment. By demonstrating vulnerability, leaders signal that taking risks and making mistakes is acceptable, thus encouraging a culture of open communication and creativity.

The enhancement of leadership through vulnerability is profound. When leaders openly share their challenges and setbacks, they create a narrative that others can relate to. This openness fosters team cohesion, as individuals feel more connected to an approachable and transparent leader.

Consider the example of a CEO who, during a company-wide meeting, candidly discussed the difficulties faced in a failed project. By sharing their missteps and the lessons learned, the CEO not only diffused a potentially tense situation but also set a precedent for honesty and growth. This vulnerability showed employees that they, too, could learn from failures, thus encouraging innovation and resilience. Such transparency breaks down barriers, allowing teams to collaborate more effectively as they no longer fear the repercussions of failure. The leader becomes a catalyst for creativity, as team members feel empowered to propose novel ideas and solutions, knowing they are supported even if their suggestions do not always succeed.

Practical exercises can prove invaluable in integrating vulnerability into your leadership style. Role-playing scenarios in leadership workshops, for instance, offer a safe space to practice expressing vulnerability in professional settings. By simulating real-life situations where openness is required, leaders can build the confidence to apply these skills in daily interactions. These exercises encourage leaders to step out of their comfort zones, fostering a deeper understanding of how vulnerability can be strategically used to enhance their influence and impact. Through these activities, leaders learn to navigate the fine line between vulnerability and oversharing, honing their ability to connect with others while maintaining professionalism.

The relationship between vulnerability and authenticity is undeniable. Authentic leadership involves being true to oneself; vulnerability is a pathway to such authenticity. When leaders allow themselves to be seen as they are, without pretense, they cultivate an environment where authenticity thrives.

Case studies of leaders who practice authentic leadership show that embracing vulnerability often leads to greater effectiveness in their leadership. Take the example of Jacinda Ardern, the New Zealand Prime Minister, whose empathetic and open approach during crises has garnered worldwide respect and admiration. Her willingness to show emotion and admit uncertainty has strengthened her connection with the public and reinforced her credibility as a leader. This authenticity, rooted in vulnerability, enables leaders to inspire loyalty and commitment, as those they lead feel genuinely valued and understood.

In embracing vulnerability, leaders not only enhance their confidence but also create a ripple effect that influences their entire organization. Vulnerability fosters a culture where individuals feel encouraged to bring their whole selves to work, driving engagement and productivity. As leaders model vulnerability, they empower others to do the same, creating a dynamic where innovation and collaboration flourish. In doing so, vulnerability becomes not merely a personal asset but a collective strength, reshaping the very fabric of leadership.

1.4 Overcoming Imposter Syndrome with Cognitive Strategies

Imposter syndrome can be a silent saboteur in the lives of many women leaders, casting a shadow over achievements and fueling the notion that success is undeserved.

This phenomenon is characterized by persistent feelings of self-doubt and the fear of being exposed as a fraud despite evident accomplishments and accolades. Symptoms often manifest as perfectionism, an inability to internalize success, and a relentless drive to overachieve, all of which can culminate in anxiety and stress.

Women in leadership often struggle with imposter syndrome, a deceptive barrier that makes it difficult to recognize their achievements. This mental trap causes them to credit success to luck or external factors rather than their own hard work and abilities. This cycle of self-doubt not only stifles professional growth but also impairs key leadership functions such as decision-making, risk-taking, and career advancement. It is imperative to acknowledge that these feelings of inadequacy are not isolated incidents but are prevalent among high-achieving women, setting the stage for a collective effort to mitigate their effects.

Combatting imposter syndrome effectively hinges on the implementation of cognitive strategies. Cognitive restructuring, a cornerstone of cognitive-behavioral therapy, emerges as a potent tool in this battle, enabling individuals to identify, challenge, and replace irrational beliefs with balanced, realistic thoughts. For instance, when faced with a challenging project, the instinctive reaction might be doubt, typified by thoughts like, " I'm not skilled enough to succeed." However, a shift towards a more empowering viewpoint, such as, "*I have the requisite skills and experience to navigate this project, and I am equipped to seek assistance when needed*," can significantly alter one's outlook. This practice of reshaping thought patterns is instrumental in diminishing the influence of imposter syndrome, thereby revealing one's true capabilities.

Incorporating positive affirmations into daily routines is an additional strategy to reinforce self-esteem. Regularly affirming one's abilities and worth through statements like "I am capable and deserving of my success" counteracts the pervasive negative self-talk characteristic of imposter syndrome. These affirmations act as reminders of one's strengths and past successes, boosting confidence and self-belief.

The narratives of women who have confronted and conquered imposter syndrome are replete with resilience and triumph. Consider the story of a notable female executive in the tech industry who candidly shared her struggles with self-doubt at a leadership conference. Despite her achievements in leading a high-performing team and driving innovation, she often questioned the legitimacy of her role. Through mentorship and the application of cognitive strategies, she began to recognize her value and fully step into her leadership identity. Her journey and those of countless other women highlight the transformative power of directly addressing imposter syndrome. Interviews and anecdotes from successful women leaders consistently emphasize the importance of acknowledging these intrusive thoughts and actively seeking support.

Mentorship is a powerful tool for overcoming imposter syndrome, offering guidance, encouragement, and fresh perspectives essential for confident leadership. Women can share experiences, gain insights, and receive constructive feedback by participating in mentorship programs and peer support groups. Mentors help identify and challenge limiting beliefs, provide reassurance, and advocate for their mentees' skills and achievements, validating their contributions. This support system not only diminishes self-doubt but also fosters a sense of empowerment and belonging. We will explore the transformative role of mentorship in greater detail in *Chapter 7*.

	**Interactive Element:** Overcoming Imposter Syndrome Journal

Please grab a notebook or journal to complete this activity.

Set aside 20–30 minutes of uninterrupted time to reflect and write.

- **Step 1: Recognize Imposter Syndrome Patterns**

Reflect on a recent situation where you experienced self-doubt or felt like a fraud. Write down:

- **The Situation:** Describe the context (e.g., a presentation, project, promotion).
- **Your Thoughts:** What did you tell yourself in that moment? Example: "I'm not good enough for this role."
- **Your Feelings:** How did you feel (e.g., anxious, stressed, fearful)?

Example Table:

Situation	Your Thoughts	Your Feelings
Leading a project team.	"I'm not skilled enough for this."	Anxiety, fear of failure.
Presenting at a leadership meeting.	"I don't belong here; they'll realize I'm not qualified."	Nervousness, insecurity, self-doubt.

- **Step 2: Cognitive Restructuring**

Now challenge the thoughts you wrote in Step 1. Answer the following questions:

- Is there evidence to support this thought?
- What past successes prove that I am capable?
- What would I say to a friend in this situation?

Replace the negative thought with a positive and realistic affirmation.

Example:

Original Thought: "I'm not skilled enough for this."

Restructured Thought: "I have successfully led projects before and have the skills and support needed to succeed here."

- **Step 3: Affirm Your Strengths**

Write down 3–5 positive affirmations that emphasize your abilities and value.

Examples:

1. "I am capable and deserving of my success."
2. "My skills and experiences make me a strong leader."
3. "I have overcome challenges before and can handle this."

Repeat these affirmations daily for a week, ideally out loud or in front of a mirror.

- **Step 4: Seek Mentorship and Support**

Identify a mentor or peer who can provide guidance and encouragement.

Reflect on the following:

- *Who in your network can offer insights or share their experiences with imposter syndrome?*
- *What specific support or feedback do you need to feel more confident?*

Write down 1–2 action steps to connect with a mentor or support group.

- Example: *"Schedule a coffee meeting with my manager to discuss my progress and get feedback."*

Step 5: Reflect on Growth

At the end of the week, revisit the situations where you applied the above steps. Reflect on:

- How did you feel after challenging your thoughts?
- What changes did you notice in your mindset or confidence?
- What will you continue doing to overcome imposter syndrome in the future?

Make this activity a regular routine to strengthen self-awareness, challenge self-doubt, and foster continuous personal growth.

1.5 Developing a Growth Mindset for Leadership Success

A growth mindset is a powerful paradigm that distinguishes leaders who see challenges as opportunities from those who view them as threats. The concept, conceived by psychologist Carol Dweck, underscores the belief that abilities and intelligence can be developed through effort, learning, and perseverance. This starkly contrasts with a fixed mindset, which holds that these qualities are static and unchangeable. While a fixed mindset often leads to avoidance of challenges and a fear of failure, a growth mindset encourages embracing challenges as pathways to improvement.

Leaders with a growth mindset understand that setbacks are not reflections of their worth but are vital components of learning and growth. They perceive effort as an avenue to mastery rather than a sign of inadequacy, and they welcome feedback as a constructive tool for development. This perspective fosters resilience, adaptability, and a relentless pursuit of excellence, which is indispensable in the dynamic leadership landscape.

Cultivating a growth mindset requires intentional effort and a willingness to challenge ingrained beliefs. One effective strategy is setting incremental goals for skill development. By breaking down large objectives into smaller, manageable tasks, leaders can focus on continuous improvement without feeling overwhelmed. This approach builds competence and boosts confidence, as each small success reinforces the belief in one's ability to grow and adapt.

Another key strategy is embracing challenges as learning opportunities. Instead of shying away from difficult situations, leaders with a growth mindset dive into them, recognizing that these experiences, however daunting, are where the most profound learning occurs. They actively seek new challenges, understanding that each offers a chance to expand their skills and perspectives. This proactive approach to learning transforms obstacles into stepping stones, enabling leaders to navigate complex environments with agility and foresight.

The impact of a growth mindset on leadership is profound, fostering resilience and adaptability in the face of adversity. Leaders who embody this mindset are better equipped to handle the uncertainties and pressures of their roles. They remain composed despite setbacks, viewing them as temporary hurdles rather than insurmountable roadblocks. This resilience inspires team confidence, creating a culture of trust and innovation. Furthermore, a growth mindset enhances adaptability, allowing leaders to pivot strategies and easily embrace change. In an era where the pace of change is accelerating, this adaptability is crucial for sustaining organizational success.

To bolster the journey toward embracing a growth mindset, a wealth of resources stands ready to guide leaders through this transformative process. Central to this knowledge repository is "Mindset: The Psychology of Success" by Carol Dweck, a seminal work that delves into the core principles underpinning a growth mindset. Dweck's insights offer a roadmap for shifting one's perspective toward embracing challenges and viewing setbacks as opportunities for growth, making it an essential read for those committed to personal and professional development.

Coursera and LinkedIn Learning emerge as premier destinations for courses tailored to fostering resilience, enhancing adaptability, and promoting a culture of continuous learning. These platforms curate content from experts across various fields, providing leaders with the tools to navigate the complexities of their roles with grace and agility. From mastering the art of constructive feedback to exploring strategies for innovative problem-solving, these courses are structured to facilitate incremental growth, enabling leaders to build on their strengths and address areas for improvement. Whether it's carving out time during a morning commute or dedicating a quiet evening to professional development, these resources adapt to the rhythms of a leader's life, making the pursuit of a growth mindset a seamlessly integrated aspect of daily living. The commitment to nurturing a growth mindset transcends mere professional advancement; it is an investment in one's potential to lead with resilience, adaptability, and vision.

	**Interactive Activity:** Growth Goal Roadmap

This activity will guide you in breaking down large objectives into smaller, achievable steps, fostering continuous improvement, and building confidence as you progress.

---

1. **Choose a Goal**
   - Identify one specific leadership skill or area you want to improve (e.g., public speaking, giving feedback, time management).
   - Write your goal in a clear, measurable way.
     - Example: "I want to improve my public speaking skills to deliver confident and engaging presentations."

2. **Break It Down**
   - Divide your goal into 3–5 smaller, incremental steps. These should be manageable and achievable within a short time frame. Example:

Goal Step	Actionable Task	Timeline
1. Research public speaking tips	Watch 2 TED Talks on effective public speaking.	By the end of this week.
2. Practice delivery skills	Record myself presenting a 5-minute topic.	Next 2 weeks.
3. Get constructive feedback	Ask a mentor or peer to review my recording.	Within 1 month.

4. Present to a small group	Volunteer to lead a small team meeting.	Within 6 weeks.
5. Reflect and refine	Identify strengths and areas for improvement.	After 6 weeks.

3. **Track Your Progress**
   - Use a journal, notebook, or digital tool to track your progress.
   - After completing each step, reflect on the following:
     o What did I learn?
     o What went well?
     o What can I improve moving forward?

4. **Adjust and Expand**
   - Once you complete your initial goal, set a new stretch goal or refine the original goal to further challenge yourself.

"We need women who are so strong they can be gentle, so educated they can be humble, so fierce they can be compassionate, so passionate they can be rational, and so disciplined they can be free."
— *Kavita Ramdas*

1.6 Celebrating Small Wins to Build Momentum

The path to leadership is often marked by significant milestones, but it is the smaller victories along the way that can truly sustain and propel us forward. Recognizing these achievements is vital to boosting both morale and confidence. This acknowledgment, however minor it may seem, can generate a ripple effect, enhancing motivation and reinforcing a positive self-image. By celebrating small successes, we affirm our progress and encourage a mindset that values growth and perseverance. This practice not only uplifts spirits but also instills resilience, which is indispensable in the challenging landscape of leadership.

Psychologically, acknowledging achievements provides a powerful boost to self-esteem and satisfaction. It activates the brain's reward system, releasing dopamine, which fosters feelings of pleasure and motivation. This chemical reinforcement encourages us to maintain the behaviors that led to success, creating a cycle of positive reinforcement that drives further achievement. Moreover, celebrating small wins can mitigate stress and reduce burnout by providing regular affirmation of our capabilities and contributions. This consistent recognition cultivates a sense of purpose and fulfillment, reinforcing the belief that our efforts are meaningful and impactful.

To effectively track progress and celebrate achievements, utilizing tools such as habit trackers and progress journals can be immensely beneficial. Habit trackers offer a visual representation of consistency and improvement, allowing us to see tangible evidence of our dedication. They help identify patterns, highlight areas of strength, and pinpoint opportunities for growth. Progress journals, on the other hand, provide a space for reflection, enabling us to document our journey, articulate our successes, and contemplate the lessons learned from challenges. These tools serve as personal archives of achievement, fostering a deeper connection with our goals and inspiring continued effort. Additionally, milestone mapping in career planning charts a clear path forward, outlining the steps needed to reach desired outcomes and celebrating each accomplished milestone along the way. This structured approach not only clarifies the path to success but also provides regular opportunities for reflection and celebration.

Creating a culture that celebrates achievements within teams can amplify the benefits of recognizing small wins. Organizing team recognition events, whether formal or informal, fosters a sense of community and belonging. These celebrations can take many forms, from a simple acknowledgment in a team meeting to a dedicated event highlighting individual and collective accomplishments. By publicly recognizing achievements, leaders reinforce the value of each team member's contributions and cultivate an environment where excellence is rewarded and celebrated. This practice strengthens team cohesion, boosts morale, and encourages a culture of mutual support and encouragement.

The compounding effect of small wins cannot be overstated. Consistent recognition of progress builds momentum, leading to significant long-term achievements. Each small victory serves as a stepping stone, gradually constructing a pathway to larger goals.

As we conclude this exploration of celebrating small wins, it is clear that this practice is not merely a fleeting acknowledgment but a strategic approach to fostering growth and success. By embracing and celebrating each step forward, we cultivate an environment where confidence and resilience thrive, paving the way for sustained achievement and fulfillment. In recognizing the power of small wins, we empower ourselves and those around us to strive for excellence, knowing that every success, no matter how small, contributes to a greater legacy of leadership.

	**Additional Ideas:** Celebrate Small Wins

Here are some ideas to celebrate small wins:

1. **Treat Yourself**

Take a moment to enjoy a reward, such as a relaxing evening with your favorite book, a self-care day (spa, skincare, or meditation), or a special coffee or meal you've been looking forward to.

2. **Document Your Progress**

Keep a "Success Journal" where you record your big and small wins and reflect on how each step brought you closer to your goal. This is an excellent tool to revisit when self-doubt creeps in.

- *Example:* "I spoke confidently during today's team meeting and shared my ideas without hesitation. I'm proud of taking that step!"

3. **Share Your Achievement**

Share your progress with a trusted mentor, friend, or colleague.

- *Example:* "I volunteered to lead a discussion this week and received positive feedback from my team!"

4. **Celebrate with Your Support Network**

Women often thrive in supportive communities. Acknowledge your win by celebrating with peers, mentors, or family members who uplift you.

- *Example:* Plan a coffee chat or virtual celebration with a group of women who inspire and motivate you.

5. **Reward Yourself with Growth Opportunities**

Invest in yourself as a celebration. Enroll in a workshop, take a course, or read a book that aligns with your growth goals. This type of celebration acknowledges your success and prepares you for future challenges.

6. **Reflect on Your Journey**

Take a moment to look back on where you started and the progress you've made. Pair this reflection with an affirmation:

- *"I am capable, determined, and growing every day."*

***Why This Matters?**

By intentionally celebrating wins, you not only acknowledge your hard work but also train yourself to see challenges as opportunities for growth. Remember, each step forward is proof of your capabilities and resilience—own it, celebrate it, and use it to propel yourself toward the next goal.

Chapter 2: Authentic Leadership Styles

2.1 Your Leadership Style

Envision a grand symphony orchestra, where each musician's individual contribution melds into a magnificent collective performance. This analogy beautifully mirrors the essence of leadership, highlighting that it's not a monolithic endeavor but rather a multifaceted composition of diverse styles, each contributing its unique strengths to the overarching goal. In the dynamic realm of leadership, the ability to adapt and incorporate a spectrum of leadership models is not merely beneficial; it is imperative for success. For women in leadership positions, recognizing and weaving these varied styles into their approach can significantly boost their effectiveness and authenticity.

As women who lead, understanding and integrating these diverse styles can enhance your effectiveness and authenticity. The traditional leadership style that prioritizes assertiveness and results has long dominated the narrative. However, the emergence of models like servant leadership and transformational leadership presents new avenues for women to lead with impact and integrity.

Servant leadership, rooted in the ethos of prioritizing the needs, growth, and well-being of team members above one's own, fundamentally shifts the traditional leadership paradigm. It is an approach where leaders are seen as stewards of their teams, emphasizing support, development, and empowerment.

This leadership style creates an environment where the focus is on nurturing each individual's potential and addressing their needs, thereby fostering a culture rich in trust, collaboration, and mutual respect. The essence of servant leadership lies in its ability to build a cohesive team dynamic where members feel genuinely valued and supported, encouraging them to contribute their best with enthusiasm and commitment.

Contrastingly, transformational leadership is characterized by its ability to inspire and motivate team members to exceed their perceived limitations and embrace growth and change. This leadership style hinges on articulating a clear, compelling vision and engaging with team members in a manner that is both charismatic and inclusive. Transformational leaders are adept at sparking innovation and fostering an adaptive, forward-thinking culture within the organization. They empower individuals by recognizing and nurturing their unique talents and capabilities, thereby encouraging them to explore and realize their full potential. This not only drives organizational progress but also cultivates a dynamic and innovative workplace atmosphere where change is not just welcomed but celebrated.

Together, servant and transformational leadership styles encapsulate a holistic approach to fostering leadership environments that are conducive to personal development, team cohesion, and organizational innovation. By embracing the principles of both styles, leaders can effectively inspire their teams, championing a culture of mutual growth, respect, and transformative change.

Diverse leadership models offer significant benefits. Each style has its place and effectiveness, depending on the context. For instance, servant leadership can be particularly effective in team dynamics that require high levels of collaboration and support. When team members feel supported and valued, their engagement and productivity increase. Transformational leadership, with its emphasis on vision and change, can be instrumental in driving innovation and motivating teams during periods of transition. Situational leadership's adaptability is crucial in organizational cultures that are dynamic and fast-paced, where the ability to pivot is essential for success. Understanding when and how to apply these diverse styles empowers you to lead effectively in a variety of contexts, enhancing both your leadership impact and the performance of your team.

Experimentation with different leadership styles is crucial to finding what aligns best with your values and personality. Consider your natural tendencies and how they align with different leadership models. Leadership style assessments, such as *Everything DiSC* and *EQi2.0*, can provide insights into your strengths and preferences, helping you identify which styles resonate most with you [†1]. By experimenting with these styles, you can develop a leadership approach that feels authentic and effective, allowing you to lead with confidence and purpose.

Examining case studies of diverse leaders provides valuable insights into the application and effectiveness of various leadership styles. Take, for example, the leadership of Angela Merkel, former Chancellor of Germany, who exemplified situational leadership by adapting her approach to the evolving political landscape. Her ability to navigate complex challenges with pragmatism and resilience made her one of the most respected leaders in the world. In the corporate realm, Indra Nooyi, former CEO of PepsiCo, demonstrated transformational leadership by driving significant growth through her visionary leadership and commitment to innovation. Her emphasis on long-term sustainability and corporate responsibility transformed the company and inspired countless women to pursue leadership roles. These leaders, among many others, highlight the power and potential of diverse leadership styles in achieving success and driving change.

Personal Reflection Exercise:

Discovering Your Leadership Style

This exercise is designed to help you reflect on your leadership experiences and determine whether **transformational leadership** or **servant leadership** aligns more closely with your values, personality, and goals. It will also help you identify ways to integrate elements from both styles into your practice.

Step 1: Recall Key Leadership Moments

Think about a recent leadership experience. It could be leading a project, mentoring a colleague, or resolving a team challenge. Answer the following questions:

Reflection Questions	*Your Answers*
What was the situation?	
How did you approach the challenge?	
What actions did you take to motivate and guide others?	
How did your team respond to your leadership?	

Step 2: Evaluate Transformational and Servant Leadership Traits

Read each statement and rate yourself on a scale of **1 to 5** (1 = Rarely, 5 = Always).

Leadership Trait	Rating (1–5)
I inspire my team with a clear vision and motivate them to reach ambitious goals. *(Transformational)*	
I focus on empowering others and helping them grow personally and professionally. *(Servant)*	
I lead by example, demonstrating the values I want my team to embrace. *(Transformational)*	
I actively listen to my team and prioritize their needs. (Servant)	
I encourage creativity and innovation to solve problems. *(Transformational)*	
I support the personal well-being and development of my team members. *(Servant)*	
I challenge others to achieve their potential and push beyond limits. *(Transformational)*	
I prioritize collaboration and make sure everyone feels heard. *(Servant)*	

Step 3: Analyze Your Scores

- Count how many statements scored **4 or 5** in each leadership style category (Transformational or Servant).

- Which style scored higher? This may indicate your natural preference.

Reflection Questions:

- What aspects of the higher-scoring leadership style resonate most with your values?
- Do the results reflect how you see yourself as a leader? Why or why not?
- Are there elements of the other style that you would like to develop further?

Step 4: Integrate Both Styles

No leadership style is one-size-fits-all. Use the space below to outline specific ways you can integrate elements of each style into your practice.

Leadership Style	*Action Plan for Growth*
Transformational Leadership	*Example: Share a bold vision in your next team meeting to inspire motivation.*
Servant Leadership	*Example: Schedule regular one-on-one check-ins to support team members' growth.*

2.2 Leading with Empathy and Emotional Intelligence

Within the complex world of leadership, the role of empathy emerges as a pivotal pillar supporting robust team dynamics and elevated morale. Empathy, by its very definition, embodies the profound skill of deeply comprehending and sharing the emotions of others. This profound understanding lays the groundwork for effective communication and synergistic collaboration, essential components of successful leadership. When leaders embody empathy, they cultivate an atmosphere where every team member feels profoundly seen and appreciated. This nurturing environment not only bolsters trust and fosters loyalty but also significantly mitigates conflict, paving the way for heightened productivity and a harmonious workplace.

Empathy transcends the mere recognition of emotions; it involves an active and considerate response to the feelings and experiences of others. Empathetic leadership inherently requires engaging in active listening. This skill demands the leader's undivided attention to the speaker, a suspension of judgment, and a thoughtful, measured response. This level of engagement demonstrates a genuine commitment to understanding and addressing team members' concerns, thereby reinforcing their value within the team.

Leadership development programs often include workshops to help leaders strengthen their empathy skills. These workshops are designed to simulate real-world situations, providing a practical and immersive platform for leaders to hone their empathic responses and communication skills. Participants are guided through a series of exercises that challenge them to step into the shoes of others, fostering a greater understanding and appreciation for diverse perspectives and experiences. These activities not only enhance the leader's capacity to connect with their team on a more meaningful level but also equip them with the tools to navigate the complexities of human emotions with grace and competence.

Through the strategic integration of empathy into their leadership approach, leaders unlock the potential to transform their teams and organizations. Empathy acts as a catalyst for creating a culture of inclusivity, respect, and mutual support, where every individual is encouraged to contribute their best. The ripple effects of such a culture are far-reaching, resulting in not only improved team performance but also a more engaging and satisfying work environment for all.

Turning to emotional intelligence (EQ) this indispensable skill forms the backbone of leadership effectiveness and informed decision-making. Emotional intelligence is comprehensive, encompassing self-awareness, self-regulation, social awareness, and relationship management. These components are crucial for adeptly navigating one's own emotional states and understanding those of others. Leaders who possess a heightened level of EQ excel in identifying their own emotional triggers and appreciating how these emotions influence their thoughts, choices, and behaviors. This profound self-awareness is instrumental, as it equips leaders to maintain their composure and resilience, even in challenging circumstances, thereby setting a constructive example for their teams.

Furthermore, EQ is central to resolving conflicts with empathy and insight. Leaders with robust emotional intelligence are skilled at uncovering the emotions underlying conflicts and addressing these issues in ways that promote resolution and harmony. Their proficiency in managing relationships and cultivating networks—essential aspects of emotional intelligence—significantly enhances their ability to inspire and influence, leading to notable improvements in organizational performance.

The process of developing empathy and EQ is an evolving journey enriched by engaging in specific, targeted exercises. Role-playing scenarios are particularly effective, offering a controlled setting in which to practice empathetic listening and emotional regulation. These scenarios mimic real-life interpersonal challenges, affording leaders the opportunity to immerse themselves in diverse perspectives and thereby deepen their empathetic understanding. Reflective journaling serves as another vital tool in this developmental journey. By documenting daily interactions and emotional responses, leaders engage in introspective analysis of their feelings and behaviors, pinpointing opportunities for growth. This reflective practice not only enhances self-awareness but also promotes a thorough exploration of one's emotional landscape, leading to increased emotional intelligence.

Through committed engagement in these exercises, leaders cultivate a deeper understanding of both themselves and their teams, fostering a leadership style that is empathetic and emotionally intelligent. The transformative impact of empathy in leadership is powerfully demonstrated through the experiences of leaders who prioritize connection and understanding.

A compelling example is a healthcare executive who fundamentally transformed her organization by making empathy a core value. Her dedication to actively listening to the needs and concerns of both staff and patients laid the groundwork for trust and a spirit of collaboration, resulting in significant improvements in patient care and employee satisfaction. This executive's empathetic approach not only boosted team morale but also ignited a culture of innovation and excellence within the organization. Testimonials from her team underscore the profound impact of her leadership, highlighting an enhanced sense of belonging and increased motivation. These accounts confirm that empathy extends beyond a 'soft skill,' emerging as a strategic asset with the power to drive meaningful organizational success and transformation.

Empathy and EQ Development Exercise:

Reflective Journaling for Leadership Growth

This exercise is designed to enhance your **empathy** and **emotional intelligence (EQ)**—two essential qualities for effective leadership. Reflecting on daily interactions will build greater self-awareness, improve emotional regulation, and strengthen your ability to connect with others.

- **Step 1: Daily Reflection Prompt**

At the end of each day, take 10–15 minutes to reflect on the following questions:

1. Describe the Interaction:

- Who was involved, and what was the situation?
- What emotions were present—both yours and the other person's?

2. Assess Your Response:

- How did you respond emotionally and verbally?
- Did your actions demonstrate empathy? Why or why not?

3. Evaluate the Outcome:

- What was the result of the interaction? Was the outcome positive, neutral, or negative?
- How did your response influence the emotions or behaviors of others?

4. Identify Lessons Learned:

- What insights did you gain about your emotional triggers and reactions?

- What could you have done differently to improve the interaction?

5. Plan for Growth:

- How will you apply what you've learned to future interactions?
- What specific behavior or strategy will you focus on tomorrow?

- **Step 2: Tracking Progress**

Weekly Review:
Review your journal entries at the end of each week and look for patterns. Use the following table to summarize key takeaways:

Key Insight	Example Interaction	Improvement Plan
Noticed I interrupted discussions	Staff meeting where I didn't allow input from a peer.	Practice active listening and pause before speaking.
Felt defensive when receiving feedback	Performance review conversation with a manager.	Focus on openness by asking clarifying questions.
Recognized a team member's frustration	Project check-in where deadlines were unclear.	Provide clearer timelines and validate concerns.

- **Step 3: Expand Your EQ Toolkit**

In addition to journaling, incorporate these practices to enhance empathy and emotional intelligence:

1. **Active Listening Practice:**
    - Pay full attention to speakers without interrupting.
    - Reflect back on what you hear to ensure understanding.

2. **Perspective-Taking Exercise:**
   o Put yourself in others' shoes before reacting to challenging situations.
   o Ask yourself: "What might they be feeling right now?"
3. **Empathy in Action:**
   o Offer support to someone facing a challenge.
   o Practice validating others' emotions without judgment.

- **Step 4: Reflect and Celebrate Growth**

Monthly Reflection:
At the end of each month, revisit your progress and celebrate wins. Reflect on the following:

- How has your ability to empathize improved?
- What specific changes have you noticed in your interactions with others?
- What area of EQ do you still want to work on?

Outcome:

By consistently practicing reflective journaling and applying insights gained, you will:

- *Develop deeper self-awareness and emotional regulation.*
- *Strengthen relationships through empathy and improved communication.*
- *Lead with emotional intelligence, fostering trust and collaboration within your team.*

2.3 Crafting Your Personal Leadership Brand

In the complex world of leadership, cultivating a personal brand transcends mere self-promotion; it is an authentic manifestation of your deepest convictions, strengths, and aspirations. Think of your leadership brand as a lighthouse, emitting a steadfast beam that illuminates your unique identity and guiding principles to the world. Far from being a mere facade, it embodies the genuine expression of your core values, distinguishing attributes, and long-term visions. A robust brand identity, underpinned by consistency in your messaging, ensures that your external persona resonates with your internal ethos. This congruence between how you present yourself and how you wish to be perceived is instrumental in building trust and establishing credibility—cornerstones of influential leadership. When your actions and decisions echo the essence of your brand, it validates your identity and amplifies your sway across your organization and your field at large.

The journey to forge your personal leadership brand is introspective and demands a clear understanding of your intrinsic motivators. Begin by delving into your personal values—the unassailable beliefs that anchor your identity. Reflect on what propels you forward, the principles you steadfastly uphold, and the legacy you aim to create. This deep-rooted self-awareness lays the groundwork for your brand. Following this, craft a mission statement encapsulating your leadership ethos and ambitions. A thoughtfully composed mission statement shines as a beacon, offering direction and imbuing your endeavors with purpose. It concisely broadcasts your vision and the distinctive value you contribute to your team and wider organization. Throughout this process, the importance of authenticity cannot be overstated. Genuine authenticity engenders trust and bolsters your credibility, which is vital for impactful leadership. Make sure your actions align with your values so that your behavior truly reflects your brand's ethos. Sidestep the pitfalls of inauthenticity, such as portraying an image at odds with your true self or modifying your brand to meet external expectations. Remember, authenticity signifies embracing your genuine self with honesty and integrity rather than pursuing an illusion of perfection.

The articulation of your leadership brand is pivotal in cementing your influence and presence. In today's digital age, social media platforms stand as powerful conduits for magnifying your voice and forging connections with a broader audience. Leverage these platforms to disseminate insights, accomplishments, and thought leadership that align with your brand narrative. It is crucial that your online persona seamlessly reflects your professional identity, ensuring consistency across all virtual touchpoints. Beyond digital outreach, networking emerges as a critical strategy for brand reinforcement. Immerse yourself in your industry's ecosystem by attending events, participating in forums, and engaging with peers in ways that resonate with your core values and areas of expertise. Networking transcends the mere expansion of your professional circle—it's about nurturing substantive relationships that mirror and bolster your brand values.

Developing a compelling leadership brand is not a static achievement but a dynamic, ongoing process that evolves in tandem with your professional journey and personal growth. This dynamic process requires ongoing self-reflection and a willingness to evolve, ensuring your brand remains impactful and relevant. Consider the narrative of a distinguished business leader who adeptly molded and communicated her brand. She commenced by identifying her foundational values of innovation and inclusivity, which steered her leadership style. Her mission statement, centered on catalyzing transformative change through diversity and collaborative effort, served as her north star. By actively engaging with her audience on social media, she shared the vicissitudes of her leadership journey—her challenges, triumphs, and learnings. Through consistent and authentic engagement, she not only solidified her reputation as a trailblazer but also galvanized others to champion the values she embodied, thereby cascading a wave of positive change.

|  | **Interactive Activity:**

Building Your Personal Leadership Brand |

This activity will guide you through defining and strengthening your personal leadership brand by aligning your values, vision, and actions.

Step 1: Identify Your Core Values

- List **3–5 values** that define your leadership approach (e.g., integrity, collaboration, innovation).

- **Reflection Question**: *What principles guide my decisions and actions as a leader?*

Example Table:

Value	Why It Matters to Me
Integrity	I believe in being honest and transparent in all dealings.
Collaboration	Working together leads to better results and inclusivity.

Step 2: Craft Your Mission Statement

- Write a **1–2 sentence mission statement** that reflects your leadership vision and goals.

Prompt:
What impact do I want to make as a leader?
Example:
"I strive to inspire and empower others to reach their full potential through collaboration, mentorship, and innovation."

Step 3: Align Actions with Values

- List **3 daily actions** that demonstrate your values in practice.

- **Reflection Question**: Do my actions consistently reflect my values and mission?

Example Table:

Value	Action
Integrity	Provide honest feedback during performance reviews.
Collaboration	Facilitate brainstorming sessions to encourage diverse input.

Step 4: Utilize Social Media to Reinforce Your Brand

- Create or update your **LinkedIn profile** to reflect your values and mission.

- **Task**: Share or comment on articles aligned with your leadership focus.

- **Reflection Question**: *What content can I share that highlights my expertise and values?*

Step 5: Engage in Networking

- Identify **three key contacts** to build or strengthen relationships with who align with your leadership goals.

- **Task**: Schedule a virtual coffee chat or networking session this month.

- **Reflection Question**: *Who can help reinforce and support my leadership journey?*

2.4 Balancing Assertiveness and Approachability

In leadership, the dual forces of assertiveness and approachability create a dynamic balance that can significantly enhance your effectiveness. Assertiveness, often misunderstood, is the ability to communicate your thoughts, needs, and boundaries clearly and confidently without infringing on the rights of others. It is not to be confused with aggression, which involves imposing one's will on others, often at the expense of their rights and feelings. In contrast, approachability is the quality that makes you accessible and open to others, inviting dialogue and collaboration. It encourages team members to share their ideas and concerns without fear of judgment or reprisal. Together, these traits form the backbone of authentic leadership, enabling you to guide with strength while remaining open and receptive.

To strike a harmonious balance between these traits, you must employ strategies that maintain the equilibrium necessary for effective leadership. Assertive communication techniques are essential tools in this endeavor. These techniques involve expressing your ideas and expectations clearly while remaining respectful and considerate. For example, the use of "I" statements can help articulate your perspective without sounding confrontational. Phrases like "I think" or "I feel" allow you to assert your position while acknowledging the other person's viewpoint, fostering a more constructive dialogue. Additionally, creating a welcoming team environment is crucial for nurturing approachability. Encourage open communication by setting aside regular times for team members to share thoughts and feedback. This practice not only builds trust but also empowers your team to contribute to decision-making processes, enhancing their sense of ownership and commitment.

The impact of balancing assertiveness and approachability on team dynamics is profound. Leaders who master this balance cultivate an environment where open communication and mutual respect thrive. By encouraging feedback loops, you create a culture of continuous improvement where team members feel valued and heard. These loops involve regularly seeking input from your team and responding to their suggestions, demonstrating that their contributions are integral to the team's success. Furthermore, leading inclusive meetings ensures that all voices are considered and respected. This inclusivity can be achieved by actively facilitating discussions, inviting quieter team members to share their insights, and ensuring that all perspectives are given equal weight. The result is a team that is cohesive, motivated, and engaged, capable of achieving remarkable outcomes.

Consider the example of a renowned business leader who is celebrated for her ability to maintain this balance. Her team members describe her as both decisive and approachable, highlighting her skill in making tough decisions while remaining accessible and supportive. In leadership workshops and training courses, she shares her experiences, emphasizing the importance of clear communication and active listening in fostering a positive team culture. Her approach has not only strengthened her leadership but also inspired her team to embrace these values, resulting in a more collaborative and innovative work environment. Her success underscores the transformative power of balancing assertiveness and approachability, illustrating how these traits can drive personal and organizational growth.

Balancing assertiveness and approachability is not a static process but a dynamic interplay that requires continuous attention and refinement. By cultivating these traits, you can lead with authenticity and integrity, inspiring your team to reach new heights. The journey to mastering this balance is one of exploration and growth, where the rewards extend far beyond personal success to encompass the collective achievements of your team. As you navigate this path, remember that assertiveness and approachability are not opposing forces but complementary strengths that, when harmonized, create a leadership style that is both powerful and effective.

2.5 Authentic Decision-Making: Aligning Choices with Values

Decisions shape not only the trajectory of our careers but also the cultures and operations of our organizations. At the heart of every impactful decision lies a set of core values. These values act as guiding principles, steering decisions toward authenticity and congruence with personal and organizational integrity. Defining these values is a crucial first step. Personal values are those deep-seated beliefs that guide your behavior and decisions. They are the principles that resonate with your sense of self and purpose. Organizational values, on the other hand, are the foundational beliefs that define a company's culture and goals. Together, these values form a framework that guides decision-making, ensuring alignment between individual actions and broader organizational objectives.

Value-based decision frameworks offer a structured approach to making decisions that reflect these core values. Such frameworks encourage leaders to evaluate options through the lens of their values, ensuring that choices align with the principles they hold most dear. The benefits of decisions rooted in values are manifold. They enhance personal integrity, as leaders who consistently make value-aligned decisions are seen as trustworthy and consistent. This integrity fosters respect and admiration from team members, enhancing leadership effectiveness. Moreover, value-aligned decisions contribute to organizational coherence.

When decisions are made in harmony with organizational values, they reinforce the company's mission and vision, creating a unified direction that guides the collective efforts of all team members. Organizations that prioritize value-driven leadership often experience increased employee engagement and loyalty, as team members are inspired by leaders who embody the values they espouse.

A structured approach can be extremely helpful in making decisions that align with your values. Decision trees and matrices are practical tools that help map out potential decisions and their consequences, allowing leaders to visualize the alignment of choices with their values. These tools provide a clear framework for evaluating options, weighing the pros and cons, and considering the impact of each choice on personal and organizational values. Reflective questioning techniques further enhance this process. By asking insightful questions—such as "Does this decision align with my core values?" or "How does this choice reflect the organization's mission?"—leaders can gain clarity and confidence in their decisions. Such reflection ensures that decisions are not made impulsively but are instead thoughtfully considered, with a focus on long-term outcomes and alignment with values.

Consider the story of a woman CEO who navigated a challenging ethical dilemma by steadfastly adhering to her values. Faced with the decision to cut costs by outsourcing jobs to a country with questionable labor practices, she chose to uphold her commitment to ethical labor standards, even though it meant higher expenses in the short term. Her decision, while challenging, reinforced her integrity and earned her the unwavering respect of her employees and stakeholders. Her leadership not only strengthened the company's reputation but also fostered a culture of trust and transparency. This example underscores the profound impact of value-aligned leadership on team morale and organizational success.

Aligning decisions with values is not merely a strategic choice; it is a testament to one's character and commitment to integrity. As you navigate your leadership path, let your values serve as your compass, guiding your decisions and actions toward authenticity and excellence.

"Real integrity is doing the right thing, knowing that nobody's going to know whether you did it or not."

— Oprah Winfrey.

Interactive Activity:

Decision Matrix Exercise

This activity will help you to apply structured decision-making tools to align choices with your values and organizational goals.

Step 1: Define Your Decision

Write down a specific decision you need to make (e.g., taking on a new project, hiring a team member, or investing resources in a particular area).

Prompt:

- *What is the core decision I'm trying to make?*
- *What values or principles must this decision align with?*

Step 2: Create a Decision Matrix

1. Identify 3–5 options you're considering.

2. Create a table with columns for criteria based on your values and goals.

3. Score each option on a scale of **1 to 5** (1 = Low, 5 = High) based on how well it meets the criteria.

Example Table:

Options	Aligns with Values	Impact on Team Goals	Long-Term Benefits	Total Score
Option 1: Hire internally	5	4	5	14
Option 2: Outsource work	3	4	3	10
Option 3: Delay decision	2	3	2	7

Reflection Questions:

- Which option scored the highest?

- Does this option align with my values and the organization's mission?

- What concerns, if any, still need to be addressed before acting?

Step 3: Reflect and Adjust

- Review the highest-scoring option.

- Make notes about possible adjustments to ensure alignment with values.

Step 4: Implement and Evaluate

- Write down 1–2 immediate steps to execute the decision.

- Set a date to revisit the decision and assess whether it achieved the intended outcome.

2.6 The Power of Storytelling in Authentic Leadership

The ancient art of storytelling holds a transformative power in leadership that transcends mere communication. It serves as a bridge, connecting vision and values to action and engagement. Stories have a unique ability to convey complex ideas in a relatable and memorable way, making them an invaluable tool for leaders seeking to inspire and influence. A compelling story is built on key elements: a clear narrative arc, relatable characters, and a resonant message. These elements work together to captivate and move audiences, embedding the leader's vision and values in the minds of those who listen. Storytelling workshops for leaders emphasize these components, providing a space to practice and refine the skill of narrative crafting, which is essential for effective leadership communication.

Personal narratives, in particular, are a powerful way to foster connection and inspire action. When leaders share their own experiences, they humanize their leadership, breaking down barriers and building trust. These stories often reflect personal challenges, triumphs, and lessons learned, offering a window into the leader's character and values. For instance, a leader might recount a pivotal moment in their career when they faced adversity but persevered through resilience and determination. This type of storytelling not only engages the audience emotionally but also illustrates the leader's principles in action, making the abstract tangible. Engaging your audience through questions or personal reflection makes storytelling more impactful, turning passive listeners into active participants.

Crafting impactful stories requires intentionality and clarity. Leaders must structure their narratives in a way that guides the audience through a journey of discovery and understanding. This involves setting the scene, introducing the challenge, and leading the audience through the resolution, all while weaving in the core message. Visuals and metaphors can enrich the storytelling experience, providing vivid imagery that deepens understanding and retention. A well-placed metaphor can illuminate complex ideas, while visuals, such as slides or props, can reinforce key points and keep the audience engaged. These techniques ensure that the story not only resonates but also leaves a lasting impression, aligning the audience's emotions and thoughts with the leader's vision.

As we conclude this exploration of authentic leadership styles, the power of storytelling stands out as a formidable tool for conveying vision and values. By integrating personal narratives and crafting impactful stories, you can connect with your audience on a deeper level, inspiring them to embrace and act upon your vision. As we move forward, consider how storytelling can enhance your leadership and amplify your impact.

"When the whole world is silent, even one voice becomes powerful." — Malala Yousafzai

CHAPTER 3: NAVIGATING WORKPLACE DYNAMICS

"Networking is not about just connecting people. It's about connecting people with people, people with ideas, and people with opportunities."
– Michele Jennae

3.1 Understanding Workplace Politics

Picture yourself at a lively office party, where conversations blend into a hum of chatter, laughter punctuates the air, and subtle exchanges shape the evening. In one corner, a group gathers around a senior executive, nodding in agreement, their words carefully chosen to leave a lasting impression. Across the room, a manager shares a quiet but strategic conversation with a colleague, fostering an alliance that could shape future projects. Meanwhile, others engage in casual discussions, unaware that these seemingly informal moments often hold just as much weight as formal meetings.

This setting mirrors the reality of workplace politics—the unspoken but powerful force shaping professional relationships and opportunities. It is not just about knowing your job or delivering results; it's about understanding the web of influence, alliances, and decision-making that quietly governs the workplace. These interactions, often happening behind closed doors or in casual encounters, determine who gets heard, who gets promoted, and who becomes an influential voice within the organization.

Workplace politics, while often met with skepticism, are an inevitable part of professional environments. They involve the strategic use of power, relationships, and influence to navigate challenges, advance initiatives, and achieve both personal and organizational goals. Those who recognize and engage in workplace politics ethically and effectively are more likely to open doors to leadership opportunities, gain visibility, and position themselves as key decision-makers. Understanding these dynamics isn't about manipulation—it's about positioning yourself with awareness, fostering meaningful connections, and learning how to advocate for yourself and others in ways that align with your values and career aspirations.

In various industries, the political landscape can differ significantly. For example, in corporate settings, hierarchical structures often dictate power, with influence concentrated among senior executives and key decision-makers. In contrast, creative industries may exhibit more fluid power dynamics, where influence is often based on creativity and innovation rather than formal titles. Understanding these landscapes is crucial for identifying where influence lies and how decisions are made. Mapping out organizational charts can provide a visual representation of formal hierarchies, highlighting key players and their roles within the organization. However, formal structures only tell part of the story. Informal influencers, those who wield power through relationships and networks, often play pivotal roles in workplace politics. These individuals may not hold official titles but command respect and influence through their connections and ability to mobilize others.

Successfully navigating workplace politics requires strategies that uphold your integrity while engaging with organizational dynamics. One key approach is building strong alliances with influential stakeholders. By establishing relationships with influential figures, you can gain support and access to opportunities that might otherwise be out of reach.

Participating in cross-departmental projects is another effective strategy, as it allows you to collaborate with a diverse range of colleagues and showcase your skills to a broader audience. These projects often involve working with teams across the organization, providing opportunities to build rapport and influence outside of your immediate circle. Engaging in these activities not only enhances your visibility but also positions you as a valuable contributor to the organization's goals.

While engaging in workplace politics can be beneficial, it is essential to maintain ethical standards in all interactions. Ethical considerations should guide your actions, ensuring that your engagement in politics is grounded in honesty and integrity. Engaging in unethical tactics like manipulating information or undermining colleagues can severely damage reputations and erode trust. Case studies of ethical decision-making in workplace politics highlight the importance of transparency and accountability. Consider the example of a manager who, faced with competing interests, chose to advocate for a decision that aligned with the organization's values despite potential backlash. This decision, though challenging, reinforced the manager's integrity and earned the respect of peers and subordinates. Conversely, unethical behavior can lead to negative outcomes, both personally and professionally. It can create a toxic work environment, hinder collaboration, and ultimately impede career advancement.

Navigating workplace politics with integrity requires a delicate balance of strategic engagement and ethical conduct. It involves recognizing the power structures within your organization, building alliances that align with your values, and maintaining transparency in all interactions. By understanding and embracing the dynamics of workplace politics, you can enhance your influence, open new opportunities, and advance your career while upholding the principles that define your leadership.

	**Interactive Activity:** Mapping Influence Exercise

This exercise helps you analyze your organization's political landscape, identify formal and informal influencers, and develop strategies to build alliances while maintaining ethical integrity.

Step 1: Identify Key Players

- Start by mapping out the **formal organizational chart** in your workplace.
- List the **key formal leaders** (e.g., managers, executives, decision-makers).
- Then, identify **informal influencers**—those who may not have a formal title but hold influence through relationships, expertise, or visibility.

Example Table:

Name	Role/Title	Formal or Informal Influence?	Strength of Influence (1–5)	Notes
Sarah (Manager)	Project Manager	Formal	4	Leads project teams and decision-makers.
John (Colleague)	Senior Analyst	Informal	5	Highly trusted by senior leadership.
Anna (Assistant)	Executive Assistant	Informal	3	Controls access to executives.

Step 2: Analyze Relationships and Influence Networks

- Draw a **network map** connecting individuals based on their relationships, influence, and communication patterns.
- Use **arrows** to indicate connections (e.g., mentorship, support, alliances).
- Highlight **strong influencers** by using thicker lines or bold arrows.

Reflection Questions:

- Who has the most influence within the organization?
- Are there alliances or power centers you need to be aware of?
- Where do you currently fit within this network?

Step 3: Evaluate Opportunities for Engagement

- List ways to **strengthen relationships** with key influencers while remaining ethical and authentic.
- Focus on **collaborative opportunities**, **mentorship possibilities**, and **shared goals**.

Example Table:

Influencer Name	Opportunity to Engage	Action Steps	Timeline
Sarah	Collaborate on upcoming projects	Offer support and share ideas during planning phases.	Next 2 weeks
John	Seek mentorship for strategic planning skills	Schedule a coffee chat to discuss career advice.	Within 1 month
Anna	Improve communication and rapport	Provide updates and express gratitude for assistance.	Ongoing

- *Step 4: Reflection and Ethical Considerations*

  - Reflect on how your approach aligns with your values and leadership style.

  - Identify ways to **build trust** without engaging in manipulation or unethical behavior.

Reflection Prompts:

- *What values must I uphold while building relationships?*
- *How can I balance influence-building with integrity?*
- *What actions demonstrate authenticity and transparency?*

- *Step 5: Action Plan for Building Influence*

Summarize your findings and create an **action plan** for strengthening alliances and navigating workplace dynamics.

Example Action Plan Template:

Goal	Specific Actions	Timeline
Build visibility with senior leadership.	Volunteer to present updates in team meetings.	Next 1–2 months
Strengthen network with peers.	Organize informal brainstorming sessions.	Bi-weekly meetings
Develop mentorship relationships	Reach out to experienced leaders for advice.	Monthly check-ins

3.2 Building Strategic Alliances and Networks

In the journey of professional growth, building strategic alliances is key to unlocking leadership opportunities. These alliances are not mere connections; they are powerful partnerships that enhance your influence and broaden your horizons. Strategic alliances can significantly impact your career by providing access to resources, insights, and networks that may otherwise remain out of reach. In today's interconnected world, the strength of these relationships often determines your ability to navigate complex organizational landscapes and seize leadership roles. The benefits of cross-functional partnerships, in particular, cannot be overstated. By collaborating with colleagues from different departments, you gain diverse perspectives and foster innovation, propelling both personal and organizational success.

Attending industry conferences and events is a key strategy for building relationships with professionals who share your interests and goals. These gatherings provide a platform for exchanging ideas, learning new trends, and forming connections that can lead to collaborative endeavors. Engaging in conversations with peers and thought leaders at such events can open doors to new opportunities and partnerships. Additionally, joining professional associations expands your network and offers access to resources and expertise that can support your career growth. These associations often host workshops, seminars, and Networking events, creating an environment where you can connect with like-minded individuals and cultivate mutually beneficial relationships. By actively participating in these communities, you position yourself as a committed and engaged professional, enhancing your visibility and credibility.

Engaging in collaborative projects is another effective approach to building strategic alliances. Collaboration fosters teamwork and encourages the sharing of knowledge and skills, leading to innovative solutions and shared successes. By working closely with colleagues on projects that align with your interests and expertise, you not only strengthen your relationships but also demonstrate your value as a team player and leader. These projects provide opportunities to showcase your skills, build trust, and establish a reputation as a reliable and capable collaborator. As you contribute to the success of collaborative efforts, you build a network of supporters and advocates who can champion your career advancement.

The role of reciprocity in Networking cannot be overlooked. Successful alliances are built on mutual benefit, where each party gains value from the relationship. Sharing resources, information, and support fosters a sense of reciprocity that strengthens professional bonds. Offering mentorship or assistance in exchange for guidance or opportunities creates a balanced dynamic where both parties benefit. This reciprocal approach ensures that relationships are sustainable and rewarding, contributing to long-term career success. By approaching Networking with a mindset of giving as much as receiving, you cultivate genuine connections that are rooted in trust and mutual respect.

There are many stories of leaders who have effectively leveraged alliances for career success. Joint ventures and collaborations have propelled many women to leadership positions by combining strengths and resources to achieve shared goals. For example, a marketing executive who partnered with a technology firm to develop an innovative product not only expanded her skill set but also gained access to new markets and resources. The alliance enhanced her influence within her organization and positioned her as a leader in her field. Testimonials from alliance partners highlight the value of these partnerships, emphasizing how collaboration and mutual support have led to career breakthroughs and personal growth. These stories illustrate the transformative potential of strategic alliances, demonstrating that the path to leadership is often paved with the support and collaboration of others.

As you navigate your own career, consider the strategic alliances you can cultivate to enhance your influence and open up new opportunities for growth. Recognize the power of cross-functional partnerships, and seek out collaborations that align with your goals and values. Embrace the principle of reciprocity and approach Networking with a mindset of mutual benefit. By building and nurturing these alliances, you can strengthen your leadership potential and propel your career to new heights. We will explore the transformative role of Networking in greater detail in *Chapter 7*.

3.3 Communicating with Impact in Male-Dominated Settings

In male-dominated environments, communication can often feel like navigating a labyrinth where every turn presents a new hurdle. Women frequently face interruptions, where their voices are overshadowed or dismissed before ideas can be fully articulated. Contributions, no matter how insightful, risk being overlooked or attributed to others, leaving many women feeling undervalued. These barriers are not merely anecdotal; they are entrenched in the dynamics of spaces where male voices have historically prevailed. Understanding these challenges is crucial for developing strategies to ensure your voice is recognized and respected.

To communicate with impact, adopting assertive speaking techniques is fundamental. This involves expressing your thoughts clearly and confidently, using "I" statements to convey your perspective without alienating others. Support your arguments with data and evidence, which can lend credibility and weight to your presentations. In meetings, prepare thoroughly by gathering relevant statistics and examples that reinforce your points. This preparation not only strengthens your position but also demonstrates your expertise, making it harder for others to dismiss your contributions. Non-verbal communication cues, such as maintaining eye contact and using open body language, further enhance your message. These cues signal confidence and authority, ensuring that your presence is felt even before you speak.

Confidence in communication is a powerful amplifier of credibility and influence. Practicing public speaking can build this confidence, providing opportunities to refine your delivery and receive constructive feedback. Consider joining groups like Toastmasters, where you can practice speaking in a supportive environment. Preparation is another key element in building self-assurance. Familiarize yourself with meeting agendas, anticipate questions, and rehearse your responses. This preparation reduces anxiety and equips you to handle unexpected challenges with poise. Confidence is not just a trait; it is a practice that grows with each successful interaction, bolstering your ability to assert your ideas and engage effectively with colleagues.

Interactive Activity:

Communication Style Assessment and Strategy Building

Effective communication is a cornerstone of leadership, influencing everything from team dynamics to career advancement. Few leaders exemplify this better than **Sheryl Sandberg**, the former COO of Facebook, whose communication style has been a key factor in her success.

Sandberg built her leadership presence in a fast-paced, male-dominated industry where clear, persuasive, and strategic communication was essential. She became known for her ability to break down complex business strategies into relatable, actionable insights. Whether presenting to executives, rallying teams, or delivering keynote speeches, she consistently balanced **assertiveness with empathy**—ensuring that her message was both impactful and inclusive.

Her approach wasn't just about speaking well; it was about **preparation, audience awareness, and confidence**. She tailored her messages to connect with different stakeholders, making her voice not only heard but respected. Sandberg's ability to communicate with clarity and conviction helped her advocate for herself, influence key decisions, and pave the way for more women in leadership.

Now, it's your turn to assess and refine your own communication style. This activity will guide you in identifying your strengths, pinpointing areas for growth, and developing a strategy to communicate with greater confidence and effectiveness. By doing so, you'll not only enhance your leadership presence but also position yourself as a strong and influential voice in your field.

Let's begin.

Step 1: Assess Your Communication Style

Rate yourself on the following statements using a scale of **1–5**:

1 = Rarely true   **5** = Always true

Statements	Rating (1–5)
I prepare thoroughly before important conversations or presentations.	
I adjust my communication style based on the audience's needs.	
I use clear and relatable language to explain complex ideas.	
I actively listen and make others feel heard during discussions.	
I balance assertiveness with empathy in difficult conversations.	
I use storytelling or personal anecdotes to make my points more impactful.	
I handle questions or criticism with confidence and composure.	

Reflection Questions:

- *Which statements scored **4 or 5**? These represent strengths in your communication style.*

- *Which statements scored **3 or below**? These highlight areas for improvement.*

Step 2: Analyze Sheryl Sandberg's Approach

Case Study Reflection:

- What aspects of Sandberg's communication style resonate with you?

- How does her balance of assertiveness and empathy inspire you to adapt your own approach?

- What preparation techniques can you adopt to strengthen your confidence and clarity?

Step 3: Create Your Communication Strategy

Instructions:
Based on the assessment and reflection, outline specific actions to improve your communication style:

Focus Area	Action Steps	Timeline
Preparation Techniques	Research audience needs before presentations.	Next presentation
Balancing Assertiveness with Empathy	Practice phrasing feedback constructively while staying direct.	Weekly meetings
Relating Complex Ideas Clearly	Use analogies or examples to simplify technical concepts.	Ongoing

Step 4: Practice and Feedback

Task:

- Select an upcoming meeting or presentation to practice your strategy.
- Record yourself or request feedback from a trusted peer or mentor.
- Use the following table to capture insights:

Strengths Observed	Areas for Improvement	Action Plan for Next Time
Clear explanations and examples.	I need to maintain better eye contact.	Focus on engaging eye contact.

Step 5: Reflect and Adjust

Reflection Questions:

- How did it feel to approach communication with greater preparation and intention?

- Did your adjustments have a noticeable impact on how others responded?

- What will you continue practicing to improve further?

3.4 Leveraging Feedback for Professional Growth

Imagine stepping into a room filled with colleagues, mentors, and industry leaders—each ready to offer insights that could shape your career trajectory. In this space, every conversation holds the potential to unlock new perspectives, highlight untapped strengths, and refine areas for growth. This is the power of constructive feedback—a vital tool that not only enhances professional development but also builds resilience and adaptability in leadership.

Feedback serves as a mirror, reflecting both accomplishments and opportunities for improvement. The most successful professionals don't just receive feedback; they actively seek it out. When approached with an open mind, constructive feedback can transform how we communicate, collaborate, and lead. It provides specific, actionable advice designed to support, refine, and elevate our skills, making it an invaluable asset in any career journey.

However, not all feedback is created equal. Constructive feedback is clear, actionable, and intended to uplift, offering solutions and guidance for improvement. In contrast, destructive feedback is often vague, overly critical, or demotivating, serving more as an obstacle than an opportunity. Learning to differentiate between the two allows you to embrace feedback that fuels progress while filtering out commentary that lacks substance or intent to support growth.

To truly leverage feedback, one must develop a mindset of continuous learning—welcoming insights from peers, mentors, and even challenges along the way. This requires confidence, self-awareness, and a commitment to professional evolution. Whether it's feedback from a performance review, a mentor's advice, or even a colleague's perspective on a recent project, each piece of input is an opportunity to sharpen your leadership skills and push your career forward.

When taken to heart and applied strategically, feedback is not just a passive response to criticism—it becomes an active tool for leadership excellence, professional growth, and long-term success.

To effectively harness the benefits of feedback, it is crucial to establish strategies for soliciting and receiving it. Setting regular feedback sessions with colleagues and supervisors creates a structured environment where insights can be shared openly. These sessions should be approached with curiosity and a genuine desire to improve, ensuring that feedback is welcomed and integrated into personal development plans. Creating an open feedback culture within your team or organization further facilitates this process. Encourage a two-way dialogue where feedback is not only given but also received with appreciation and consideration. This culture fosters trust and transparency, allowing for honest and constructive exchanges that benefit all parties involved. Embracing feedback as a continuous process rather than a one-time event ensures that learning and growth remain at the forefront of your professional journey.

Once feedback is received, the next step is to transform it into actionable improvement plans. This involves developing personal development goals that align with the insights gained from feedback. These goals should be specific, measurable, and time-bound, providing a clear roadmap for growth and development. Implementing changes based on feedback requires commitment and perseverance, as it often involves stepping out of your comfort zone and embracing new challenges. However, the rewards of this process are substantial, leading to enhanced skills, increased confidence, and greater professional success. By viewing feedback as a valuable resource, you can continually refine your abilities and adapt to the ever-evolving demands of the workplace.

	Exercise:
	Giving and Receiving Constructive Feedback for Growth

This exercise is designed to help you effectively **gather and provide constructive feedback**, identify areas for improvement, and create an **action plan** to foster personal and professional growth.

Step 1: Gather Feedback

1. Identify **3–5 trusted sources** (colleagues, mentors, managers) from which to request feedback.

2. Ask **specific questions** to ensure actionable responses:

    o   *What is one thing I do well that I should continue?*

    o   *What is one area where I could improve?*

    o   *How do you perceive my leadership or communication style?*

    o   *Can you share an example of a recent situation that stood out to you?*

Table Template for Feedback Collection:

Feedback Source	Key Strengths Highlighted	Areas for Improvement	Example Provided
Manager	Strong communication in meetings.	Improve follow-ups to ensure clarity.	"Last project update lacked task deadlines."
Peer	Effective collaborator and team motivator.	Delegate more to avoid burnout.	"You handled too many tasks yourself."

Step 2: Provide Constructive Feedback

1. Practice delivering feedback using the **SBI Model** (Situation, Behavior, Impact):

    o **Situation** – Describe the specific context.

    o **Behavior** – Focus on observable actions, not assumptions.

    o **Impact** – Explain how it affected you or the team.

Example:

"In yesterday's meeting (Situation),

you interrupted several times while others were sharing ideas (Behavior).

It made it difficult for some team members to contribute (Impact)."

2. Use the following **Checklist for Giving Feedback**:

- Be **specific** and avoid vague comments.

- Focus on **behavior**, not personality.

- Offer **solutions** and highlight **positives** alongside areas for improvement.

Reflection Prompt:

- *How did the person respond to your feedback?*

- *Did the feedback lead to a productive discussion or actionable outcome?*

Step 3: Take Action for Improvement

Use the feedback received to develop a clear improvement plan.

Action Plan Template:

Feedback Received	Action Steps	Timeline	Resources Needed
Improve follow-ups for project clarity.	Create a follow-up template and send summaries after each meeting.	2 weeks	Email template, task tracking app.
Delegate tasks more effectively.	Identify tasks to delegate and assign clear responsibilities.	1 month	Team collaboration tools.

Step 4: Review Progress and Reflect

Revisit your feedback and action plan regularly to track progress and adjust as needed.

Progress Tracking Template:

Goal	Current Status	Next Steps
Improve follow-ups for project clarity.	Using templates, team communication improved.	Add deadlines to follow-up emails.
Delegate tasks more effectively.	Delegated 3 tasks; the team is managing well.	Identify more opportunities for delegation.

Reflection Prompts:

- *What has improved since applying feedback?*
- *What challenges did you face, and how did you address them?*

3.5 Handling Criticism and Turning it into Opportunity

Navigating the world of professional feedback requires distinguishing between criticism and constructive feedback, as each serves different purposes and impacts. Constructive feedback is characterized by its intention to guide and improve. It is specific, actionable, and focuses on behavior rather than personal attributes. For instance, a suggestion to enhance presentation skills with concrete examples is constructive. In contrast, destructive criticism often lacks specificity and can feel personal, aiming to undermine rather than uplift. Recognizing these differences is crucial in responding appropriately. When faced with criticism, it's vital to assess whether it offers valuable insights or simply reflects the critic's biases. Such discernment allows you to approach feedback strategically, accepting constructive advice while disregarding baseless negativity.

Managing criticism effectively involves a set of skills that turn potential setbacks into opportunities for growth. Emotional regulation is the foundation of this process, enabling you to maintain composure and respond thoughtfully rather than react impulsively. Techniques such as deep breathing and mindfulness can help manage the initial emotional response to criticism, allowing for a more measured approach. Seeking clarification and context is another key strategy. By asking questions to understand the critic's perspective, you can gain insights into their observations and intentions. This approach not only clarifies the feedback but also demonstrates your commitment to improvement. Reflective listening practices further enhance this process, as they involve actively listening to the feedback, paraphrasing it, and confirming your understanding. This practice ensures that you fully grasp the essence of the criticism and can address it constructively.

Criticism, when reframed, can serve as a powerful catalyst for personal and professional development. By viewing criticism as an opportunity rather than a threat, you can uncover underlying lessons that contribute to growth. For example, criticism about time management skills may highlight the need for better prioritization and planning. Embracing this feedback as a chance to refine these skills can lead to increased efficiency and effectiveness. This perspective shift transforms criticism from a source of frustration into a valuable learning tool. By identifying the constructive elements within criticism, you can set goals and implement changes that drive self-improvement and career advancement. This proactive approach fosters resilience and adaptability, essential traits for navigating the complexities of professional life.

Consider the stories of leaders who have turned criticism into success, demonstrating the transformative power of embracing feedback. One notable example is a senior executive who faced harsh criticism for her management style. Instead of dismissing the feedback, she sought mentorship and engaged in leadership coaching sessions to address the concerns raised. Through introspection and targeted development, she transformed her approach, ultimately earning recognition for her leadership effectiveness. This case study illustrates how criticism, when approached with an open mind, can lead to personal transformation and professional success. Anecdotes from leadership coaching sessions further affirm this potential. Participants often recount how constructive criticism provided clarity and direction, enabling them to hone their skills and achieve their leadership goals.

In the ever-evolving landscape of professional development, handling criticism with poise and turning it into an opportunity is a skill that sets successful leaders apart. By differentiating between types of feedback, employing strategies for effective management, and embracing criticism as a tool for growth, you can navigate challenges with confidence and emerge stronger and more capable. Through this lens, criticism becomes not a barrier but a stepping stone toward achieving your full potential.

3.6 Cultivating a Culture of Collaboration and Inclusion

In today's workplace, collaboration and inclusion are more than just aspirational goals; they are fundamental components of a thriving organizational culture. Collaboration involves working together towards common goals, utilizing the diverse skills and perspectives of each team member. Inclusion ensures that all individuals, regardless of their backgrounds, feel valued and empowered to contribute their unique insights. Together, these principles create an environment where creativity and innovation flourish. Diverse teams bring a wealth of experiences and viewpoints, leading to more comprehensive problem-solving and decision-making. Research consistently shows that organizations embracing diversity and inclusion outperform their counterparts, achieving higher levels of employee satisfaction and retention.

To foster collaboration, leaders must actively implement strategies that encourage teamwork and dismantle silos. Team-building activities are an effective way to strengthen bonds among colleagues, promoting trust and open communication. These activities can range from structured workshops to informal gatherings, each designed to build rapport and understanding.

Encouraging cross-departmental projects further enhances collaboration by bringing together individuals with different expertise and perspectives. These projects break down barriers, fostering a culture of unity and shared purpose. Establishing open communication channels is also vital. Regular team meetings, feedback sessions, and digital platforms for collaboration ensure that information flows freely and that everyone has a voice. By creating an environment where communication is open and transparent, leaders lay the groundwork for effective collaboration.

Leaders play a pivotal role in promoting inclusion. They set the tone for organizational culture by modeling inclusive behaviors and championing diversity initiatives. Diversity and inclusion training programs are an essential tool for educating employees about the importance of these values and equipping them with strategies to implement them. These programs raise awareness of unconscious biases and provide practical skills for fostering an inclusive workplace. Leading by example is equally crucial. Leaders who actively demonstrate inclusive practices—such as soliciting input from all team members, recognizing diverse perspectives, and addressing bias—reinforce the expectation that inclusion is a shared responsibility. By embodying these values, leaders inspire others to follow suit, creating a ripple effect throughout the organization.

As we conclude our exploration of workplace dynamics, it becomes evident that cultivating a culture of collaboration and inclusion is integral to organizational success. These principles foster environments where individuals feel valued and empowered, driving innovation and growth. In the forthcoming chapter, we will delve into the strategies for achieving work-life balance, exploring how leaders can support their teams in harmonizing professional and personal responsibilities.

Chapter 4: Mastering Work-Life Balance

"Don't confuse having a career with having a life."
— Hillary Clinton

4.1 Establishing Boundaries

Imagine a tightrope walker poised high above the ground, balancing with precision and grace. The tension of the rope beneath her feet mirrors the delicate equilibrium many women strive to achieve between their professional and personal lives. This balancing act is not just about managing time; it's about setting boundaries that allow you to thrive in both arenas without sacrificing your well-being. As a woman in leadership, maintaining this balance is crucial for sustaining your energy and effectiveness. Yet, the path to achieving it can often feel elusive. Setting clear boundaries is a fundamental step in navigating this complex landscape.

Boundaries act as the guardrails that protect your time and energy, helping you delineate between work and personal life. They ensure that you allocate time for both professional responsibilities and personal rejuvenation, preventing burnout and enhancing overall well-being.

Implementing boundaries within your professional sphere means transparent communication and consistent application. A practical measure is establishing specific hours dedicated to work-related communications, delineating when you are available for meetings or responses and when you are not. Similarly, creating designated "no work" zones within your home environment reinforces these boundaries. These zones can be physical spaces explicitly reserved for relaxation, such as a home office with a closing door, or temporal boundaries, like a rule against checking emails after a certain hour. Adopting these strategies not only preserves your time but also sets a positive example for boundary-setting in your workplace, cultivating a culture of respect and mutual consideration.

Prioritizing tasks demands a strategic mindset, focusing on the most significant activities. The Eisenhower Box, an effective decision-making tool, aids in categorizing tasks by their urgency and importance, helping you identify which tasks warrant immediate action and which can be deferred, delegated, or dropped entirely. Additionally, weekly planning sessions are instrumental in maintaining this focus. Allocating time to plan your week ensures that you prioritize tasks that have the most substantial impact, encompassing both professional assignments and personal commitments. This balanced approach to time management aligns your daily endeavors with your overarching objectives, providing a clear direction for your efforts and keeping you centered on what truly matters.

The ability to say 'no' is vital to maintaining a work-life balance. Turning down non-critical commitments conserves your energy and prevents you from spreading yourself too thin. Practicing this skill through role-playing scenarios can bolster your confidence in safeguarding your time.

Establishing a personal 'no' policy further solidifies this stance. This policy entails setting specific criteria for accepting or declining requests, ensuring your choices align with your priorities. This structured approach enables you to make decisions supporting your well-being and career success.

Reflecting on your personal priorities is crucial to ensure your actions align with your goals and values. Engaging in regular reflection helps assess whether your commitments are in sync with your core values and aspirations. Journaling exercises centered around these values can offer profound insights into what is genuinely important to you. Documenting your reflections creates a tangible record of your priorities, guiding your decisions and activities. Conducting quarterly reviews of your priorities allows you to evaluate your progress toward your objectives and adjust your focus as necessary. This reflective practice guarantees that your endeavors continue to align with your evolving priorities, enabling you to navigate the complexities of work and personal life with intentionality and clarity.

4.2 Delegation: Empowering Your Team and Yourself

In leadership, delegation emerges as a pivotal skill that enhances productivity and fosters team members' growth and development. It is a strategic process that involves entrusting tasks to others, allowing you to focus on higher-level responsibilities while enabling your team to build new skills and increase their contributions to the organization.

Effective delegation is not merely about offloading tasks; it is about empowering your team, instilling confidence, and promoting a sense of ownership and accountability. As a leader, mastering delegation allows you to harness the collective strengths of your team, leading to greater efficiency and innovation.

Successful delegation starts with a clear framework, beginning with identifying which tasks can be delegated. Consider which tasks do not require your specific expertise and can be entrusted to others. This might include routine administrative tasks or projects that offer opportunities for team members to learn and grow. Once tasks are identified, the next step is matching them with the appropriate team members. This requires understanding each team member's strengths, skills, and development needs. Delegating tasks that align with these attributes not only ensures successful completion but also contributes to the individual's professional growth. Setting clear expectations and outcomes is crucial. Communicate the objectives, deadlines, and any specific requirements clearly, ensuring that team members have a comprehensive understanding of the task at hand. This clarity provides a roadmap for success and minimizes the risk of misunderstandings or errors.

Empowering team members through delegation has numerous benefits. It boosts morale by demonstrating trust in their abilities, encouraging them to take initiative and contribute more actively. When team members feel valued and empowered, they are more likely to engage with their work and seek out opportunities for further development. This empowerment leads to skill enhancement, as team members are exposed to new challenges and responsibilities. Success stories abound in teams that have thrived through effective delegation. For example, a marketing team that was given the autonomy to plan and execute a campaign not only achieved outstanding results but also developed new creative strategies that became a standard for future projects. Such stories highlight the transformative impact of delegation in fostering a culture of innovation and collaboration.

Despite its benefits, delegation can present challenges, particularly related to trust and control. Many leaders struggle with the fear of losing control and the desire to micromanage, which can undermine the delegation process. Overcoming these tendencies requires a shift in mindset. Recognize that delegation is an opportunity for growth both for you and your team. By relinquishing control, you allow team members to develop their capabilities and take ownership of their work. Building trust through open communication is essential. Regular check-ins and feedback sessions can provide assurance and support, allowing you to guide team members without overstepping. This communication fosters a collaborative environment where team members feel supported and confident in their abilities.

Addressing common delegation challenges often involves self-reflection and adjustment of leadership styles. Leaders must acknowledge their own reluctance to delegate and work to build a culture of trust and empowerment within their teams. By focusing on the strengths and potential of each team member, you can create a supportive environment where delegation becomes a natural and effective process. As you build trust and open communication, you lay the foundation for successful delegation, empowering your team to thrive and contributing to the overall success of the organization.

 **Interactive Exercise:**

Mastering Delegation for Leadership Growth

This exercise will help you to develop the skill of effective delegation, empowering your teams while overcoming common challenges such as trust and control.

Step 1: Self-Reflection on Delegation Habits

Reflect on your current delegation practices using the following prompts. Write your responses in a journal or notebook.

Reflection Prompts:

- *What tasks do I typically delegate?*
- *Do I find it challenging to delegate certain tasks? Why?*
- *What fears or concerns do I have about delegating to my team?*
- *How confident am I in my team's ability to handle delegated tasks?*

Step 2: Delegation Planning Framework

Follow the steps below to create a delegation plan for an upcoming project or responsibility. Use the table provided to organize your thoughts.

    1) **Identify Tasks to Delegate:** List 2–3 tasks that do not require your direct expertise or that offer growth opportunities for your team members.

2) Match Tasks to Team Members: Consider each team member's strengths, skills, and areas for development.

3) Set Clear Expectations: Define objectives, deadlines, and key deliverables.

4) Monitor Progress and Provide Feedback: Schedule regular check-ins to offer support and ensure alignment.

Delegation Plan Table (Example):

Task	Assigned Team Member	Skills Needed	Expected Outcome	Deadline	Check-in Date
Update project timeline	Sarah	Time management, detail-oriented	Accurate timeline for project tracking	2 weeks	Weekly review
Design campaign graphics	Emily	Creativity, design tools	High-quality, visually appealing graphics	3 weeks	Midway feedback
Draft client proposal	John	Writing, client focus	Persuasive and clear proposal	1 week	The day before the due date

Step 3: Building Trust and Communication

Practice open communication with your team to build trust and empower them. Use the following strategies:

- **Check-In Without Micromanaging:** Schedule brief updates to ensure progress while allowing team members autonomy.
- **Feedback Focused on Growth:** Provide constructive feedback that highlights strengths and suggests areas for improvement.

Reflection Questions After Communication:

- *How did I show trust in my team's abilities?*
- *What positive outcomes did I notice from empowering them?*

Step 4: Overcoming Delegation Challenges

Identify one challenge you face when delegating and develop a strategy to overcome it.

Challenge	Proposed Solution
Fear of losing control	Focus on the benefits of delegation and schedule structured check-ins.
Reluctance to delegate important tasks	Start by delegating small portions of key tasks to build trust.

Step 5: Celebrate Delegation Wins

Recognize the positive outcomes of your delegation efforts. Reflect on how your team grew and how it impacted your leadership.

4.3 Time Management Techniques for Busy Leaders

In the fast-paced realm of leadership, effective time management is akin to wielding a finely honed instrument. It enables you to navigate the daily influx of demands with precision and poise. Among the arsenal of time management methods, the Pomodoro Technique stands out as a tool for enhancing focus. This method involves working in concentrated bursts, typically 25 minutes, followed by a short break. These intervals, or "Pomodoros," help maintain high levels of concentration and stave off fatigue. By structuring your workday in this way, tasks that once seemed insurmountable become manageable as focus and productivity are optimized.

Another powerful strategy is time blocking. This involves scheduling your day into distinct blocks of time, each dedicated to specific tasks or activities. By assigning a purpose to each segment of your day, you create a structured schedule that minimizes distractions and enhances efficiency. Time blocking provides a visual roadmap of your day, ensuring that important tasks receive the attention they warrant. Additionally, the 80/20 Rule, or Pareto Principle, is a valuable guideline for prioritization. This principle suggests that 80% of results often stem from 20% of efforts. By identifying and focusing on high-impact activities, you can allocate your time and resources more effectively, maximizing productivity and minimizing wasted effort.

In addition to these techniques, various apps and tools can help improve time management. Productivity tools like Trello and Asana offer platforms for organizing tasks and tracking progress. These apps allow you to create task lists, set deadlines, and monitor your workflow, providing a clear overview of your responsibilities. Analyzing time logs can also offer valuable insights into how your time is spent. By reviewing these logs, you can identify patterns, recognize areas for improvement, and adjust your strategies to enhance productivity. This data-driven approach to time management empowers you to make informed decisions about where to invest your efforts, ensuring alignment with your goals.

Flexibility, however, remains integral to effective time management. In the ever-changing landscape of leadership, adaptability is crucial for handling unforeseen tasks and changes in priorities. Managing interruptions with strategies like scheduling specific times for checking emails or handling unexpected issues can help you stay focused while allowing for necessary adjustments. Building buffer times into your daily schedule is another effective approach. These buffer periods allow for unforeseen delays or opportunities, ensuring that your schedule remains flexible and realistic. By embracing adaptability, you can navigate disruptions with agility and maintain momentum toward achieving your objectives.

As you incorporate these time management techniques into your leadership practice, remember that the goal is not to fill every moment with activity but to ensure that your time aligns with your priorities and values. By balancing structure with flexibility, you can achieve greater efficacy and fulfillment in your leadership role.

	Activity: Time Management Mastery Using Priorities, Values, and Proven Techniques

This activity helps you integrate time management strategies, including the **Pomodoro Technique, 80/20 Rule**, and alignment with **priorities and values**, into a structured workflow inspired by tools like Trello and Asana.

Step 1: Define Priorities Aligned with Values

1. List your **top priorities** for the day or week.

2. Reflect on how each priority aligns with your core values and professional goals.

Template:

Priority	Why It Matters (Values/Goals)	Deadline
Complete project report	Demonstrates accountability and leadership.	End of the week.
Prepare client pitch	Aligns with innovation and building partnerships.	Tomorrow.

Step 2: Organize Tasks with Trello/Asana-Style Workflow

1. Divide your tasks into **three categories**:

    o **To-Do:** Tasks you need to start.

    o **In Progress:** Tasks you're actively working on.

    o **Done:** Tasks you've completed.

2. Write tasks on sticky notes or in a digital tool and move them between columns as progress is made.

Example Workflow Table:

To-Do	*In Progress*	*Done*
Research for a client pitch.	Draft client presentation	Completed weekly check-ins
Review project report feedback.		

Step 3: Use the Pomodoro Technique

1. Choose a task from your **To-Do** list.

2. Set a timer for **25 minutes** and work on the task without interruption.

3. Take a **5-minute break** after the timer ends.

4. Repeat for four Pomodoro cycles, then take a longer **15–30 minute break**.

Reflection Prompt:

- Did the Pomodoro Technique help you stay focused?
- Which tasks benefited most from this approach?

Step 4: Apply the 80/20 Rule

1. Review your tasks and identify the **20% of activities** that will produce **80% of your results**.

2. Prioritize those tasks at the start of your day or week.

Template:

Task	Impact (High/Low)	Effort (High/Low)	Priority (Yes/No)
Prepare client presentation	High	Low	Yes
Organize team meeting	Low	High	No

Step 5: Align Time Blocks with Priorities and Values

1. Schedule your tasks in time blocks, ensuring high-priority tasks are aligned with your energy levels.

2. Reflect on how your time use aligns with your values and long-term goals.

Template:

Time Block	Task	Aligned Value/Goal
9:00–10:00 AM	Prepare client presentation	Innovation and accountability.
10:30–11:00 AM	Review project report	Leadership and attention to detail.

4.4 Creating a Supportive Home Environment

A nurturing home environment serves as a critical refuge, blending personal wellness with professional achievement. It's in this safe haven that the emotional support of family provides a protective shield against leadership pressures, laying down a solid foundation of strength, motivation, and resilience. Such a setting enables you to rejuvenate and recalibrate, cultivating equilibrium and promoting a sense of purpose. The support of loved ones doesn't just offer solace but also fortifies your resolve to face external challenges with confidence and grace. This foundation of security and positive reinforcement is essential for sustaining your leadership efficacy and well-being.

To cultivate a positive and harmonious home atmosphere, consider establishing family routines and rituals that foster connection and predictability. These rituals can range from shared meals, where everyone gathers to discuss their day, to weekend activities that promote bonding and fun. For example, a Friday family movie night or a Sunday morning hike can create shared experiences that foster a sense of belonging and unity. Additionally, designing shared spaces dedicated to relaxation and interaction enhances the nurturing quality of the home. Cozy reading nooks, family game corners, or multi-use spaces for leisure activities can provide opportunities for relaxation and meaningful interaction, reinforcing the bonds that sustain a harmonious family life.

Open communication within the home is paramount for addressing and resolving conflicts. Encouraging dialogue ensures that concerns are aired promptly, preventing misunderstandings and fostering mutual respect. Family meetings can serve as a platform for discussing issues, setting expectations, and planning for the future. These gatherings promote transparency and collaboration, allowing each member to voice their thoughts and contribute to collective decision-making. By using conflict resolution techniques such as active listening, empathetic responses, and collaborative problem-solving, families can navigate disagreements with patience and understanding. This approach not only resolves immediate issues but also strengthens the family unit, preparing it to face future challenges with solidarity and mutual trust.

For families juggling professional and personal responsibilities, especially those with children, achieving balance requires intentional effort and collaboration. Sharing duties with your spouse and implementing strategies to enhance efficiency at home can make a significant difference.

In my own experience, sharing responsibilities with my husband has been transformative. We encountered challenges, especially when tasks were forgotten or left undone, leading to frustration and unnecessary stress. To address this, we implemented a strategy that has brought structure and peace to our home. We created a shared Gmail account accessible on both our phones, using its calendar feature to schedule important family or child-related events. With notifications enabled, my husband now receives reminders directly on his cellphone, significantly increasing the likelihood that tasks are completed on time. This simple yet effective system has reduced miscommunication and allowed us to focus more on enjoying time together as a family. This tip will inspire you to find solutions tailored to your family dynamics.

Another efficiency measure we adopted was online grocery shopping. Previously, we would spend 2–3 hours in the supermarket, often buying more than necessary. With groceries delivered directly to our door, we've saved time, minimized unnecessary purchases, and gained better control over our expenses. This small change has greatly impacted our ability to focus on what truly matters.

In addition, I recommend the book "The 5 Love Languages" by Gary Chapman. This insightful guide helped me better understand how to express love in ways that resonate most with each family member. During busy weekdays filled with work and parenting duties, we can still ensure we show love based on what they value, not just how we perceive love. Whether it's words of affirmation, acts of service, quality time, gifts, or physical touch, discovering and applying these languages strengthens connections even in the busiest seasons.

Actionable Insights for a Supportive Home:

- **Establish Clear Routines:** Create rituals that foster connection, like shared meals, regular family check-ins, or dedicated time for fun activities.
- **Use Technology for Organization:** Leverage shared calendars and task management apps to coordinate responsibilities effectively.
- **Streamline Household Tasks:** Identify areas where you can save time, such as online shopping or meal prep services, to focus on family and personal goals.
- **Prioritize Communication:** Regularly discuss challenges and successes as a family, ensuring all members feel heard and valued.
- **Invest in Relationship Building:** Read resources like "The 5 Love Languages" to deepen understanding and strengthen bonds.

By cultivating a supportive home environment, sharing responsibilities, and focusing on efficient systems, you create a sanctuary that sustains your well-being and empowers you to thrive in leadership and beyond.

4.5 Practicing Mindfulness for Stress Reduction

In a high-pressure leadership environment, stress can often seem unavoidable. However, integrating mindfulness into your daily routine can serve as an effective tool for stress reduction and mental clarity. Mindfulness is being fully present and engaged at the moment without distraction or judgment. It involves a heightened awareness of your thoughts and feelings, allowing you to manage stress more effectively. Mindfulness meditation, a fundamental aspect of this practice, encourages you to focus on your breath and observe your thoughts as they pass, fostering a sense of calm and balance. This meditative practice clears the mind and enhances your ability to respond thoughtfully to challenging situations, improving both personal well-being and leadership effectiveness.

Incorporating mindfulness into your daily life need not be an elaborate endeavor. Simple practices such as breathing exercises can be seamlessly integrated into your routine to enhance focus and reduce stress. For instance, taking a few minutes daily to engage in deep breathing can help center your thoughts and calm your mind. Mindful walking, another accessible technique, involves paying attention to the sensations of walking, such as the feel of your feet on the ground and the rhythm of your breath. Similarly, mindful eating encourages you to savor each bite, focusing on the flavors and textures of your food. For those seeking guided support, meditation apps like *Calm* and *Headspace* offer structured sessions that make mindfulness both accessible and adaptable to your schedule, providing a variety of meditations suited to different needs and preferences.

The impact of mindfulness on leadership is profound, influencing decision-making and emotional regulation. By cultivating mindfulness, leaders can develop greater clarity and focus, enhancing their ability to evaluate complex situations impartially. This practice encourages a thoughtful approach to challenges, fostering a calm and measured response that benefits both the leader and their team. Case studies of mindful leadership practices reveal that leaders who prioritize mindfulness are better equipped to handle stress, make informed decisions, and maintain emotional equilibrium. Testimonials from women leaders who have embraced mindfulness attest to its transformative effects, highlighting improvements in both personal resilience and professional acumen.

For those interested in deepening their mindfulness practice, numerous resources are available to support your exploration. Books such as *"The Miracle of Mindfulness"* by Thich Nhat Hanh offer insights into the philosophy and practice of mindfulness, providing guidance for integrating it into your life. Courses and workshops, available both in-person and online, offer interactive experiences that deepen your understanding and application of mindfulness techniques. Mindfulness retreats provide a more immersive experience, offering dedicated time and space to focus on your practice and gain new perspectives. These resources provide a foundation for continued growth and learning, enabling you to harness the benefits of mindfulness fully.

As you consider integrating mindfulness into your routine, remember that it is a personal practice that can be tailored to suit your unique needs and lifestyle. Whether through meditation, mindful breathing, or other techniques, mindfulness offers a path to greater clarity, balance, and resilience in your leadership role.

4.6 Self-Care Routines for Sustained Energy

In the demanding landscape of leadership, self-care is not a luxury but a necessity. It's the foundation upon which energy, resilience, and clarity are built. Self-care extends beyond the physical realm, encompassing mental, emotional, and spiritual well-being. It's about nurturing every aspect of the self to sustain the energy required for effective leadership. Imagine your well-being as a reservoir; if not regularly replenished, it eventually runs dry, leaving you depleted and vulnerable to burnout. This is why self-care is crucial. It acts as a buffer, fortifying you against the relentless demands of both professional and personal responsibilities.

Creating personalized self-care routines requires an understanding of what genuinely replenishes and energizes you. Physical exercise and balanced nutrition are cornerstones of a healthy lifestyle. Regular physical activity, whether it's a morning jog, yoga, or a dance class, invigorates the body and sharpens the mind. Nutrition plays a vital role, too. A diet rich in nutrients fuels your body and brain, enhancing your capacity to lead effectively. Beyond physical health, engaging in hobbies and creative pursuits offers an outlet for expression and relaxation. Whether it's painting, gardening, or playing an instrument, these activities provide a mental escape, reducing stress and fostering creativity. Scheduling regular downtime is equally important. Setting aside time for rest and leisure ensures that you recharge, maintaining the stamina needed for sustained productivity.

Self-care is intrinsically linked to leadership effectiveness. Leaders who prioritize their well-being tend to exhibit higher levels of productivity and creativity. Studies have shown that self-care practices, such as regular exercise and stress management, enhance cognitive function and decision-making skills. Consider leaders who have publicly advocated for self-care, like Arianna Huffington, who emphasizes the importance of sleep and meditation. Her experiences underscore the profound impact of self-care on professional performance. By maintaining personal well-being, leaders not only perform better but also inspire their teams to adopt similar practices, creating a culture of health and balance within the organization.

A holistic approach to self-care addresses the interconnected aspects of well-being—physical, emotional, and mental. Integrating practices like yoga and meditation can provide this balance, offering both physical benefits and mental clarity. These practices encourage mindfulness, promoting stress reduction and emotional regulation. They help cultivate a centered mindset, enhancing your ability to lead with composure and empathy. Additionally, seeking support from mental health professionals is a vital aspect of self-care. Therapy or counseling can offer valuable insights and coping strategies, helping you navigate the complexities of leadership with confidence. This support fosters resilience, enabling you to face challenges with a healthy mindset.

As we reflect on the broader themes of work-life balance, it's clear that self-care is not an isolated practice but a fundamental component of effective leadership. It empowers you to sustain energy and maintain focus, ensuring you are at your best both professionally and personally. As you move forward, consider how a commitment to self-care can enhance your leadership capacity and overall quality of life.

In the next chapter, we will explore how advancing your career authentically intertwines with the principles of self-care and balance, paving the way for sustainable success.

Your Voice Matters!

Share Your Thoughts, Inspire Others.

As you explore *The Power of Women in Leadership*, take a moment to reflect on what has resonated with you. Your insights can inspire other women to embrace their leadership potential.

A short review—whether it's a favorite lesson, a powerful story, or an "aha" moment—can encourage others to take this step, just as you have. Your voice fuels a movement of women supporting one another in leadership.

Thank you for being part of this conversation.

Together, we lead authentically and boldly!

Chapter 5: Advancing Your Career Authentically

"If you can't find a path, make one." — *Eleanor Roosevelt*

5.1 Career Roadmap

The path to authentic career advancement can often feel like navigating a dense forest. Each path seems to diverge, and the way forward is not always clear. For many women, the leadership journey is filled with unique challenges and opportunities that require careful planning and strategic thinking. Crafting a personalized career advancement plan is not merely about setting ambitious goals; it's about creating a tailored roadmap that aligns with your aspirations and strengths. This plan becomes your compass, guiding you through the complexities of career progression and ensuring that each step you take resonates with your true self.

Setting clear career goals is the base of effective career planning. It begins with visualizing success and defining what that looks like for you. Vision boards are a powerful tool in this process, allowing you to articulate your dreams and aspirations visually. By creating a collage of images and words that represent your desired outcomes, you create a tangible representation of your goals, serving as a constant reminder of what you are working toward. Alongside this, goal setting should encompass both long-term and short-term objectives. Long-term goals outline your career ambitions, such as achieving a leadership position or transitioning into a new industry. Short-term goals, on the other hand, are the actionable steps that lead you toward these long-term aspirations. By breaking down your career trajectory into manageable milestones, you can maintain focus and motivation as you progress.

A structured framework for developing your career advancement plan involves setting *SMART* goals. These goals are **S**pecific, **M**easurable, **A**chievable, **R**elevant, and **T**ime-bound, ensuring that each objective is clear and attainable. For instance, rather than setting a vague goal like "improve leadership skills," you might specify, "enroll in a leadership development course within the next six months." This specificity allows for precise measurement and evaluation, ensuring that your goals remain aligned with your career vision. Identifying the key skills and competencies needed to achieve these goals is another critical component. This requires an honest assessment of your current capabilities and a strategic plan for acquiring new skills. Whether through formal education, workshops, or on-the-job training, continuous learning is essential for career advancement. Furthermore, creating a timeline for achieving milestones helps organize your efforts and provides a sense of urgency and direction.

The role of self-assessment in planning cannot be overstated. Regular evaluation of your progress ensures that you remain adaptable and responsive to changing circumstances. Journaling about your accomplishments and challenges is a self-reflection exercise that provides valuable insights into your growth and areas for improvement.

Additionally, utilizing feedback from mentors and peers provides external perspectives that can guide your course corrections. Feedback is a gift that offers clarity and direction, helping you refine your plan and strategies.

Aligning your career advancement plan with personal values is crucial for maintaining integrity and authenticity. Value alignment check-ins ensure that your professional pursuits do not come at the cost of personal beliefs and principles. By regularly reflecting on how your goals align with your core values, you can make informed decisions that honor your true self. Case studies of value-driven career paths highlight the success of individuals who have prioritized integrity over short-term gains. These leaders have navigated their careers with a focus on ethical considerations and personal fulfillment, demonstrating that it is possible to achieve success without compromising one's values.

	**Interactive Element:** Vision Board Creation Exercise

This exercise will help you visualize your career goals and aspirations, serving as a daily reminder of the path you're on and the success you aim to achieve.

Step 1: Prepare for Your Vision Board

What You'll Need:

- A physical board (e.g., corkboard, poster board) or a digital platform (e.g., Canva, Pinterest).
- Magazines, printed images, or online visuals.
- Scissors, glue, tape, or pins for a physical board.
- Inspirational quotes, words, or affirmations that resonate with your goals.

Reflection Questions:

- *What does success look like for me?*
- *What career goals and aspirations do I want to achieve?*
- *Which values, skills, or habits will help me reach these goals?*

Step 2: Gather Inspiration

1. Search for images, words, or quotes that resonate with your career vision.

Examples: A photo of a professional woman in a leadership role, words like *"Empowerment"* or *"Resilience,"* or a quote like *"Success is no accident."*

2. Consider categories such as:

- **Career Goals:** Promotions, leadership roles, new skills.

- **Work-Life Balance:** Family time, travel, hobbies.

- **Personal Growth:** Confidence, communication, emotional intelligence.

Step 3: Assemble Your Vision Board

1. Arrange your chosen images, words, and quotes on your board or digital platform.

- Place the most important or inspiring elements at the center.

- Group similar themes together (e.g., skills development, leadership aspirations).

2. Use a layout that feels intuitive and inspiring to you.

Optional Additions:

- Include a **timeline** for achieving specific goals.

- Add space for **new elements** as your goals evolve.

Step 4: Display and Reflect

- Place your vision board in a location where you'll see it regularly, such as your workspace or bedroom.

- Take 5 minutes each morning or evening to reflect on your vision board:

    - *What small steps can I take today to move closer to these goals?*

Step 5: Revisit and Update

- Every 3–6 months, revisit your vision board.
- Reflect on your progress:
  - *What goals have I achieved?*
  - *Do my aspirations still align with my current values and priorities?*
- Update your board with new goals or inspirations.

5.2 Navigating Promotions and Negotiations

In the competitive landscape of today's workforce, securing a promotion requires more than just doing your job well. It's about strategically showcasing your achievements and demonstrating your readiness for the next level of responsibility. Documenting your accomplishments is a first and crucial step. Maintain a detailed record of your contributions, highlighting quantifiable successes such as increased sales, successful project completions, or cost savings. This documentation not only serves as evidence of your performance but also builds a compelling narrative of your progression and impact.

"Let us never negotiate OUT OF FEAR. But let us never FEAR TO NEGOTIATE." — John F. Kennedy

Creating a business case for your promotion is equally important. This involves aligning your contributions with the organization's goals and illustrating how your advancement would benefit the company. Presenting this case to decision-makers requires clarity and confidence, underscoring your readiness to take on greater challenges.

When it comes to negotiations, whether it's for a salary increase, benefits, or a new role, preparation is your strongest ally. Begin by thoroughly understanding your worth in the industry. Conduct market research to gather data on salary benchmarks for your position and experience level. This information empowers you to enter negotiations with confidence backed by concrete figures.

Developing negotiation skills through practice can also be beneficial. Role-playing negotiation scenarios with a trusted colleague or mentor can simulate real-life discussions, helping you refine your approach and responses. This preparation enhances your ability to articulate your value clearly and assertively, increasing the likelihood of a favorable outcome. Additionally, preparing for negotiation discussions by anticipating potential objections and rehearsing your responses ensures that you remain composed and persuasive throughout the process.

Women often encounter specific challenges in negotiations, including gender bias and the potential for being perceived as overly aggressive or demanding. Overcoming these barriers requires a blend of confidence and strategy. Building negotiation confidence begins with acknowledging your achievements and embracing your strengths. Remember that you are negotiating not just for yourself but for the value you bring to the organization. Adopting a collaborative approach, rather than an adversarial one, can also be effective. Frame the negotiation as a conversation about mutual benefits, highlighting how your proposals align with the company's objectives. By doing so, you shift the focus from personal gain to collective success, reducing potential resistance and fostering a more positive dialogue.

5.3 Building Influence Without Compromise

Within the professional world, influence operates as a significant power that transcends the simple authority attached to one's job title. Influence is the ability to inspire and guide others, to shape decisions, and to cultivate an environment where ideas flourish. Unlike authority, which relies on hierarchy and position, influence is earned through respect, trust, and the consistent demonstration of integrity. It is the invisible thread that weaves through successful leadership, creating a tapestry of collaboration and innovation. In today's interconnected world, influence is not only desirable but necessary for effective leadership, as it enables you to navigate complex dynamics and foster a culture of engagement and empowerment.

To build influence authentically, you must lead by example, embodying the principles and values you wish to see in others. Demonstrating integrity in your actions fosters trust and respect, essential components of influence. When you act with transparency and honesty, you create an environment where others feel safe to express their ideas and take risks. This trust is built through consistent actions that align with your words, reinforcing your credibility and reliability. Moreover, networking with intention and authenticity enhances your influence. By cultivating genuine relationships and seeking meaningful connections, you expand your reach and impact. Authentic networking is about building mutually beneficial relationships where both parties contribute and grow.

The impact of influence on career growth is significant, opening doors to new opportunities and collaborations. Influential leaders are often sought after for high-stakes projects and strategic initiatives, as their ability to inspire and mobilize teams is highly valued.

Profiles of women who have risen through influence reveal common traits: a commitment to integrity, a focus on building relationships, and a passion for empowering others. These leaders demonstrate that influence is not about asserting control but about inspiring collective action toward a shared goal.

Reflecting on your personal influence style is crucial for understanding and refining your approach to leadership. Self-assessment of influence methods allows you to identify your strengths and areas for growth. Consider how you engage with others, how you communicate your vision, and how you build trust and rapport. Do you lead with empathy and understanding? Are you consistent in your actions and words? These reflections provide insights into your influence style, guiding you toward more effective leadership. Exercises to enhance personal influence can further support this growth. Engaging in activities that challenge your communication skills, emotional intelligence, and relationship-building abilities can strengthen your influence over time.

5.4 The Role of Sponsorship in Career Growth

In the complex terrain of today's professional world, grasping the unique roles of mentorship and sponsorship in career growth is essential. While both relationships are pivotal, they serve distinct purposes. Mentorship involves guidance and advice, often focusing on personal development and skill enhancement. A mentor is someone who shares their expertise and provides support as you navigate challenges. In contrast, sponsorship is an advocacy relationship. A sponsor goes beyond advice; they actively promote and endorse you for opportunities. They use their influence to open doors and place your name in discussions where it matters most. This distinction is crucial because while mentors prepare you for career advancement, sponsors propel you into it.

Finding and securing a sponsor requires strategic networking within your organization. Identify individuals who hold positions of influence and whose values align with yours. Building relationships with potential sponsors starts with demonstrating your value proposition. Articulate how your skills and achievements align with the organization's goals. Engage with them through professional platforms, meetings, or company events, showcasing not only your competence but also your commitment to shared objectives. This approach establishes you as a proactive and strategic professional, increasing the likelihood of gaining their advocacy. Sponsors are more likely to invest in those who show potential for growth and alignment with organizational success.

The benefits of sponsorship extend far beyond immediate career advancement. Sponsors provide access to high-visibility projects and strategic initiatives that can enhance your profile and reputation. These opportunities can accelerate your career trajectory, allowing you to showcase your capabilities on a larger stage. Stories of individuals who have advanced through sponsorship illustrate the profound impact of this relationship.

To maximize the sponsorship relationship, set clear objectives for what you hope to achieve through sponsorship and communicate these goals to your sponsor. This clarity ensures that both parties are aligned and working toward the same outcomes. Regular communication and updates with your sponsor are essential for maintaining the relationship. Provide progress reports and seek feedback, demonstrating your commitment to growth and development. This ongoing dialogue keeps your sponsor informed and engaged, reinforcing their investment in your success.

Being proactive also involves taking the initiative. Identify areas where you can contribute to your sponsor's projects or goals, offering your skills and insights. This collaboration not only strengthens your relationship but also demonstrates your value as a strategic partner. By consistently delivering results and showcasing your potential, you reinforce your sponsor's confidence in your abilities. This proactive approach transforms the sponsorship from a passive relationship into a dynamic partnership, driving both your career growth and the success of the projects you undertake.

In this dance of career advancement, sponsorship serves as a powerful catalyst. It bridges the gap between potential and opportunity, providing the platform and support needed to ascend to new heights in your professional journey.

5.5 Advocating for Yourself and Others

In the journey of professional growth, self-advocacy is a vital skill that empowers women to navigate their careers confidently. It means actively highlighting your achievements, showcasing your capabilities, and ensuring your contributions receive the recognition they deserve. Communicating your value is essential, and one powerful way to do this is by crafting a strong elevator pitch—a concise, impactful statement that conveys who you are, what you bring to the table, and why your work matters. This brief yet impactful speech should encapsulate who you are, what you do, and what you bring to the table, all within the span of an elevator ride. This is your opportunity to leave a lasting impression at networking events, team meetings, or casual gatherings. Additionally, documenting and sharing your successes within your team amplifies your impact. By regularly communicating your achievements, you highlight your contributions and inspire others to recognize their accomplishments and advocate for themselves.

Advocacy requires strategic engagement in various professional settings. Speaking up in meetings and discussions is vital, ensuring that your ideas and insights are heard and considered. This involves preparing your points in advance, articulating them clearly, and engaging respectfully with others' contributions. Building a strong personal brand reinforces your reputation as a dedicated and capable professional. You create this brand through consistent performance, integrity, and a commitment to excellence in everything you do. Engaging in professional development opportunities is another powerful strategy. By continually expanding your skills and knowledge, you demonstrate a commitment to growth and leadership, enhancing your credibility and influence within your organization. These strategies collectively empower you to advocate effectively, positioning you as a leader in your field.

Supporting others in their professional journeys is equally essential. Advocacy extends beyond self-promotion; it involves fostering an empowering work environment where peers and colleagues thrive. Mentoring and supporting junior team members is a powerful way to contribute to this environment. By sharing your experiences and insights, you help others navigate challenges and seize opportunities, building a culture of collaboration and mutual support. Initiating advocacy groups or networks within your organization can further amplify this impact. These groups create shared learning and empowerment platforms, enabling individuals to connect, collaborate, and advocate for one another's growth and success. Through these collective efforts, you contribute to a workplace where everyone's voice is heard and everyone's potential is realized.

Taking Action: Practical Steps to Advocate for Yourself and Others

To implement these strategies, start by crafting your personal elevator pitch. Take a few moments to reflect on your achievements, skills, and aspirations. Write a concise and compelling summary you can share confidently when opportunities arise. Practice delivering this pitch with a trusted colleague or mentor, refining it until it feels authentic and impactful. Remember, your pitch is about communicating your value, building connections, and leaving a lasting impression.

Next, commit to actively participating in meetings and discussions. Before each meeting, prepare at least one idea or insight you can contribute. Practice articulating your points clearly and confidently, and don't hesitate to follow up with questions or suggestions that add value to the conversation. Over time, this consistent engagement will build your reputation as a thoughtful and proactive contributor.

Finally, identify opportunities to support others in their professional journeys. Offer mentorship to a colleague or initiate a collaborative project highlighting your team members' strengths. If your organization doesn't have an advocacy group or network, consider starting one. Even a small group focused on shared growth and learning can create a ripple effect of empowerment and collaboration. By taking these steps, you advocate for yourself and create an environment where others can thrive alongside you.

Example of an Elevator Pitch:

Scenario: Networking at a Professional Event

"Hi, I'm [Your Name], and I specialize in [Your Field/Industry]. I'm passionate about helping organizations [solve a specific problem or achieve a specific goal]. For example, in my current role as a [Your Position] at [Your Company], I've led projects that [describe a key achievement, e.g., improved efficiency by 20%, increased customer satisfaction, etc.]. I pride myself on combining [your key skills or qualities, e.g., strategic thinking and collaboration] to deliver impactful results. I'm particularly interested in opportunities to [specific interest, e.g., expand into new markets, drive innovative solutions, etc.]. I'd love to hear more about your work and any challenges you face in this area."

Scenario: Internal Presentation at Work

"Hello, I'm [Your Name], and as [Your Position], I focus on [specific area, e.g., improving operational efficiency]. Recently, I [specific example of success, e.g., implemented a new tool that reduced project timelines by 15%]. I'm passionate about finding innovative ways to solve problems. I always seek ways to collaborate on initiatives that align with our company's goals."

Key Elements of a Great Elevator Pitch:

1. **Introduction:** Start with your name and current role or expertise.

2. **Highlight Your Value:** Share a key skill, passion, or achievement demonstrating your impact.

3. **Be Concise:** Keep it under 30 seconds and to the point.

4. **Engage the Listener:** End with a question or invitation to continue the conversation.

5.6 Leveraging Online Presence for Career Opportunities

Effectively navigating the digital world can greatly boost your career opportunities. A strong online presence acts as a magnet, drawing in opportunities that match your professional goals. By building your brand online, you create a compelling narrative that showcases your expertise and sets you apart in your field. Digital platforms like LinkedIn provide a stage for you to showcase your skills, experiences, and aspirations to a global audience. This visibility is crucial in today's interconnected world, as employers and collaborators often turn to online profiles to gain insights into potential colleagues and partners. Engaging actively and strategically on these platforms can open doors that might otherwise remain closed.

Building and maintaining an online presence requires deliberate effort and strategy. Begin by optimizing your LinkedIn profile, ensuring it reflects your professional journey and achievements accurately. A compelling headline and a well-crafted summary can capture your attention and convey your value. Regularly update your profile with new skills, certifications, and projects to keep it fresh and relevant. Participating in industry-related online communities can further bolster your visibility. Engage in discussions, share  insights, and connect with thought leaders to expand your network. These interactions not only enhance your profile but also position you as a knowledgeable and engaged professional in your field. Sharing thought leadership content, such as articles or blog posts, further establishes your expertise and invites collaboration. Contributing valuable content demonstrates your knowledge and commitment to advancing your industry.

While cultivating an online presence, authenticity remains paramount. The digital world can often blur the lines between personal and professional identities, making it easy to present an inauthentic version of oneself. However, maintaining an online persona that aligns with your values is crucial for building trust and credibility. To build a strong and credible online presence, ensure that your digital brand reflects your true self. Avoid the common mistake of creating an image that feels inauthentic by aligning your online activities with your core values. From the tone of your posts to the content you share and the conversations you engage in, consistency is key. Authenticity not only fosters genuine connections but also builds trust and confidence among peers and potential collaborators. When you present yourself truthfully, you create a lasting impression that strengthens your professional credibility.

As we conclude this chapter, it is evident that a strong online presence is a critical component of career advancement in today's digital age. By strategically building and maintaining your digital footprint, you enhance your visibility and open doors to new opportunities. This chapter has explored the foundational elements of advancing your career authentically, providing the tools and insights necessary to navigate your professional path with confidence. As we progress, the subsequent chapter will focus on navigating through systemic barriers, providing you with additional strategies to flourish in your leadership journey.

CHAPTER 6: OVERCOMING SYSTEMIC BARRIERS

"The question isn't who's going to let me; it's who is going to stop me."– Ayn Rand.

6.1 Barriers in the Workplace

As you walk into your office, imagine the invisible walls that might exist around you, crafted over decades by policies and norms that subtly dictate who thrives and who merely survives. These are systemic barriers entrenched within organizational structures and cultures, affecting your career trajectory and those of countless women before and after you. Systemic barriers are the deeply rooted obstacles that perpetuate inequality in the workplace, often going unnoticed but wielding significant influence over those who ascend to leadership roles and those who remain stagnant.

These barriers manifest in various forms, from policies that inadvertently disadvantage certain groups to cultural norms that uphold inequality. Policies such as rigid work hours and lack of parental leave disproportionately affect women, especially those balancing career and family responsibilities. Additionally, promotion criteria that favor traditional leadership styles can marginalize women who lead differently yet effectively. Cultural norms, like the expectation for women to prioritize personal life over career, further entrench these barriers, reinforcing stereotypes that limit opportunities for advancement. These systemic issues create an environment that, while appearing impartial, systematically favors those who conform to established norms.

To identify these barriers, you can start by conducting workplace audits or assessments. These audits involve a thorough examination of company policies, practices, and culture to uncover biases and inequities. By analyzing hiring practices, pay scales, and promotion criteria, you can pinpoint areas where systemic barriers exist. Employee feedback through surveys also provides invaluable insights. These surveys allow you to gather perspectives across different levels of the organization, revealing the lived experiences of employees who may face these barriers. By encouraging honest feedback, you create an opportunity to gain a comprehensive understanding of how systemic issues manifest and impact your workplace.

Systemic barriers have profound implications for career advancement. They act as invisible ceilings that stall career progression and limit opportunities for growth. Documenting and analyzing these barriers is crucial for driving change. By creating a barrier analysis report, you systematically capture the obstacles you and others face, providing a foundation for advocacy and reform. Identifying patterns in organizational behavior helps to highlight systemic issues that may not be immediately apparent. For instance, if promotion data reveals a consistent gender imbalance, this pattern can point to underlying biases in promotion criteria or evaluation methods.

Interactive Element:

Workplace Systemic Barrier Checklist

Step 1: Policy Review

- Examine workplace policies for inclusivity. Focus on areas such as parental leave, flexible work arrangements, promotion criteria, and diversity initiatives.

- Reflect on whether these policies are consistently applied and accessible to all employees.

Checklist Example:

Policy	Is It Inclusive? (Yes/No)	Areas for Improvement
Parental Leave Policy	Yes	Ensure equitable application for all genders.
Flexible Work Arrangements	No	Introduce more options for hybrid work.
Promotion Criteria Transparency	No	Clarify criteria and communicate widely.

Step 2: Cultural Norms Assessment

- Identify workplace norms that may perpetuate gender stereotypes or create unequal expectations. Examples include perceptions around work-life balance or expectations of after-hours availability.

Reflection Prompts:

- *Are there unspoken norms that discourage work-life balance?*

- *Are certain roles or tasks disproportionately assigned based on gender?*

Example Table:

Norm	Impact on Equity	Suggested Change
Expectation to work overtime regularly	Limits opportunities for caregivers.	Promote flexible deadlines when possible.

Step 3: Employee Feedback

- Conduct surveys or informal check-ins with colleagues to gather insights into their experiences with workplace equity. Use open-ended and multiple-choice questions.

Sample Questions:

- *Do you feel supported in pursuing leadership opportunities?*

- *Have you experienced or witnessed barriers to career advancement?*

- *What changes would you like to see to make the workplace more inclusive?*

Step 4: Data Analysis

- Analyze hiring, retention, and promotion data for patterns of inequality or bias. Look for disparities in gender representation, pay equity and leadership demographics.

Template:

Metric	Current Data	Observed Patterns	Recommendations
Gender Representation	60% men, 40% women	Fewer women in senior leadership roles.	Develop mentorship programs for women.

| Promotion Rate by Gender | Men: 20%, Women: 10% | Disparity in promotions. | Review and clarify promotion criteria. |

Step 5: Document Findings and Take Action

•   Compile your findings into a concise report. Highlight key barriers, areas for improvement, and actionable recommendations.

•   Present the report to leadership or your DEI (Diversity, Equity, Inclusion) team to advocate for change.

Reflection Prompts:

•   *What barriers surprised you the most?*

•   *What immediate steps can you take to address these barriers?*

•   *How can you contribute to a culture of inclusivity in your workplace?*

Outcome:

By completing this activity, you will:

1.   Gain a deeper understanding of systemic barriers in your workplace.

2.   Identify actionable steps to foster inclusivity and equity.

3.   Contribute to meaningful organizational change, paving the way for a more supportive environment for all employees.

6.2 Strategies for Challenging Gender Bias

Gender bias remains a significant barrier to career progression, shaping workplace dynamics in both obvious and subtle ways. It affects hiring, promotions, and everyday interactions, often placing additional hurdles in front of women.

In hiring, women frequently face stricter scrutiny, working harder to prove their qualifications than men. For example, a woman may be overlooked for a leadership role—not due to a lack of competence but because of outdated assumptions about her ability to lead. Similarly, bias in promotions can result in women being passed over for advancement or given fewer opportunities to develop leadership skills.

Beyond hiring and promotions, gender stereotyping influences job assignments, further limiting women's career growth. They are often steered toward administrative or supportive roles. At the same time, strategic or technical positions are perceived as better suited for men. This not only restricts individual career paths but also reinforces stereotypes that prevent organizations from fully leveraging diverse talent. Recognizing and addressing these biases is essential for creating a more equitable workplace where all professionals can thrive based on their skills and potential.

Eliminating gender bias requires intentional action to challenge ingrained perceptions and practices. One critical step is implementing unconscious bias training, which helps employees and managers recognize their biases and understand how these biases influence decision-making. By raising awareness, organizations can take proactive steps toward fostering a more equitable environment.

Another effective approach is advocating for gender-neutral job descriptions. Ensuring that job postings are free from gendered language and biased criteria attracts a wider and more diverse pool of candidates, promoting fairness in recruitment while reinforcing an inclusive culture. Regular reviews of hiring and promotion practices can help organizations identify and address biased processes. Establishing clear, objective criteria for advancement—focused on skills and performance rather than subjective factors—is essential for fair and merit-based evaluations.

While these changes can be challenging, they are necessary steps toward reducing gender bias and building a more inclusive workplace.

Leadership plays a pivotal role in shaping workplace culture and addressing gender bias. Leaders have the power to set expectations, drive initiatives, and create accountability for equitable practices. One impactful approach is setting clear diversity goals, ensuring that inclusion is not just a talking point but a measurable priority. These goals should be specific, trackable, and aligned with the organization's values, making diversity and inclusion a fundamental part of the company's mission.

To reinforce these efforts, leaders must lead by example. Demonstrating equitable practices in decision-making, ensuring diverse representation in meetings, and actively supporting the professional development of women within the organization send a strong message that bias will not be tolerated. Leaders who champion diversity and inclusion create a ripple effect, inspiring others to follow their lead and fostering an environment where all employees feel valued and supported.

By committing to these strategies, organizations can dismantle the barriers that hold women back and pave the way for a workplace where talent, rather than gender, determines success.

6.3 Promoting Diversity and Inclusion from Within

Imagine a workplace where diversity and inclusion are not just aspirational goals but foundational elements woven into the fabric of the organizational culture. Such environments thrive on the richness of varied perspectives, fostering innovation and enhancing decision-making. Organizations that embrace diversity benefit from a broader range of ideas and solutions, as individuals from different backgrounds bring unique insights and experiences to the table. This diversity in thought leads to more comprehensive problem-solving and creativity, driving competitive advantage and organizational success. A diverse workplace is not only more dynamic but also more adaptable, as it draws on the collective strengths of its people to navigate complex challenges.

To promote diversity effectively, it is crucial to implement practical strategies that enhance inclusion within teams. One such approach is creating inclusive recruitment processes. This involves broadening the criteria used in hiring to focus on skills and potential rather than traditional qualifications that may inadvertently exclude diverse candidates. Organizations can attract a wider range of applicants by eliminating biases in job descriptions and ensuring diverse  hiring panels. Additionally, supporting Employee Resource Groups (ERGs) plays a significant role in fostering inclusion. These groups provide a platform for employees to connect, share experiences, and advocate for change within the organization. ERGs enhance a sense of belonging and empower employees to contribute to diversity initiatives, amplifying their voices and perspectives.

Inclusive leadership is pivotal in championing diversity and inclusion initiatives. Leaders set the tone for organizational culture and have the power to drive meaningful change. By encouraging diverse talent development programs, leaders can ensure that all employees have access to opportunities for growth and advancement. These programs should focus on mentoring, skill-building, and leadership development, providing pathways for diverse employees to reach their full potential. Sponsoring diversity events and workshops is another effective way for leaders to demonstrate their commitment to inclusion. These events raise awareness, promote understanding, and celebrate diversity, reinforcing the organization's values and fostering a culture of respect and collaboration. Leaders who actively participate in and support these initiatives clearly communicate that diversity and inclusion are priorities, inspiring others to follow their example.

Promoting diversity and inclusion from within requires a commitment to continuous improvement and a willingness to challenge the status quo. It involves recognizing the value that diverse perspectives bring and taking deliberate actions to ensure that all voices are heard and respected. By fostering an inclusive environment, organizations can unlock the full potential of their workforce, driving innovation, collaboration, and success. As a leader, you have the power to champion these initiatives and create a workplace where diversity is celebrated and inclusion is the norm. Embrace this opportunity to make a lasting impact, not only for your organization but for the individuals who call it their professional home.

6.4 Building Allies in Leadership Positions

In the complex environment of organizational leadership, allies are invaluable. They serve as champions for change, supporting initiatives that promote equity and inclusion. Allies in leadership roles wield significant influence over organizational policy, shaping the direction and priorities of the company. Their support can accelerate systemic change, breaking down barriers that might otherwise persist unchallenged. When leaders commit to being allies, they use their positions to advocate for diversity, equity, and inclusion, reinforcing the importance of these values in every aspect of the organization. Their influence can shift organizational priorities, ensuring that policies and practices are inclusive and equitable.

Building alliances with leaders who can support your efforts to drive change begins with identifying potential allies through strategic networking. Seek out leaders who share your values and goals, as they are more likely to support initiatives that align with their own vision for the organization. Engage with these leaders by attending industry events, participating in professional groups, and building relationships through meaningful conversations. During these interactions, focus on finding  common ground and shared objectives, as these are the foundations upon which strong alliances are built. When leaders see that their values are reflected in your goals, they are more likely to lend their support, creating a partnership that can drive meaningful change.

Once potential allies are identified, the next step is to engage them effectively. Approach leaders with a clear plan that outlines the systemic changes you wish to implement and how these changes align with the organization's overall mission. Present data and case studies that illustrate the benefits of diversity and inclusion, such as improved employee satisfaction and increased innovation, to build a compelling case for support. Demonstrating how these initiatives can enhance organizational performance makes it easier for leaders to see the value in supporting them. It's also important to emphasize the mutual benefits of collaboration, highlighting how their involvement can enhance their own leadership impact while supporting the organization's mission.

Allies play a crucial role in advocacy, amplifying the voices of those who might otherwise go unheard. They use their influence to promote systemic change, advocating for policies and practices that foster a more inclusive workplace. Leaders who champion diversity initiatives often do so by using their platform to highlight the contributions of underrepresented groups, ensuring that diverse perspectives are considered in decision-making processes. This advocacy not only raises awareness but also drives action as allies push for changes that create a more equitable environment. By supporting allies in leadership positions, you can ensure that your efforts to drive change are supported at the highest levels, increasing the likelihood of success.

6.5 Leading by Example: Inspiring Systemic Change

The power of leading by example cannot be overstated, especially when it comes to driving systemic change within an organization. *As a leader, your actions speak louder than words*, setting the tone for the organizational culture and influencing those around you. When you embody the values you wish to promote, such as inclusivity, equity, and transparency, you become a role model for your team and colleagues. This form of leadership is about more than just policy or rhetoric; it involves demonstrating through everyday actions that these values are important and integral to how the organization operates. By consistently modeling inclusive behavior, you inspire others to adopt similar practices, creating a ripple effect that can transform the workplace culture over time.

Embodying these values requires a deliberate and conscious effort. Begin by consistently reinforcing inclusive policies within your team and across the organization. This could involve ensuring that all voices are heard during meetings, promoting diverse hiring practices, or supporting employees in pursuing leadership opportunities. When you make inclusivity a visible and tangible part of your leadership, you help create an environment where everyone feels valued and respected. Publicly supporting diversity initiatives is another powerful way to lead by example. This could mean sponsoring diversity workshops, participating in employee resource groups, or advocating for inclusive practices at the executive level. By taking these actions, you demonstrate a commitment to systemic change, encouraging others to follow suit and prioritize diversity and inclusion in their own roles.

The ripple effect of exemplary leadership can lead to widespread organizational change. When colleagues witness a leader actively supporting diversity and inclusivity, it creates a culture of accountability and inspiration. Others are encouraged to adopt similar practices, gradually shifting the organizational culture toward one that values and celebrates diversity. This ripple effect can lead to increased employee engagement, improved morale, and a more innovative and collaborative work environment. As more individuals begin to lead by example, the cumulative impact can result in significant cultural shifts, breaking down barriers and paving the way for systemic change.

Transformative leaders throughout history have demonstrated the power of leading by example, leaving lasting legacies and inspiring systemic change. One such leader is Ursula Burns, the former CEO of Xerox, who broke barriers as the first Black woman to lead a Fortune 500 company. Her leadership was marked by a commitment to diversity and inclusion, which she exemplified through her actions. By advocating for diverse hiring practices and supporting mentorship programs, Burns set a precedent for future leaders. Her influence extended beyond Xerox, inspiring other organizations to prioritize diversity in their leadership ranks. Another example is Mary Barra, the CEO of General Motors, who has championed diversity and inclusion as key components of the company's strategy. Under her leadership, GM has implemented initiatives to promote gender equality and foster an inclusive workplace culture. Barra's dedication to these values has not only transformed GM but also set a standard for the automotive industry as a whole.

These leaders exemplify the profound impact of leading by example on an organization and its culture. Through their actions, they have inspired systemic change, breaking down barriers and creating opportunities for others to follow in their footsteps. As you navigate your leadership role, consider the values you wish to embody and how you can lead by example to inspire similar transformations within your own organization. By doing so, you not only contribute to a more inclusive and equitable workplace but also leave a lasting legacy that can inspire future generations of leaders.

Chapter 7: Building Strong Networks and Mentorship

"A mentor is someone who allows you to know that no matter how dark the night, in the morning, joy will come. A mentor is someone who allows you to see the higher part of yourself when sometimes it becomes hidden to your own view." –Oprah Winfrey

7.1 Authentic Networking

Consider the vast expanse of a garden. Each plant, distinct yet interconnected, thrives through a network of roots, sharing nutrients and supporting one another's growth. This imagery parallels the importance of networking in your professional journey. Networking transcends the mere exchange of business cards; it is about forging genuine connections that nourish both personal and career development. As women in leadership, authentic networking offers a pathway to create lasting relationships and mutual support systems, which are invaluable in navigating the complexities of professional life. Unlike transactional contacts, where interactions are fleeting, authentic networking emphasizes depth and sincerity, fostering alliances that endure and evolve over time.

Building long-term relationships requires a strategic and intentional approach. Authentic networking thrives on mutual benefit and shared goals, where each party invests in the other's success. This lays the groundwork for trust and collaboration, creating a network that can provide support, advice, and opportunities throughout your career. To cultivate these relationships, approach networking with a clear purpose. Attending events with defined objectives helps focus your efforts and ensures that interactions are meaningful. Rather than seeking to connect with as many people as possible, prioritize quality over quantity. Engage with individuals whose values and interests align with yours, fostering connections that are both genuine and impactful.

Effective networking also hinges on the art of active listening. By giving your full attention to others, you demonstrate respect and interest, which are foundational to building rapport. Active listening involves more than hearing words; it requires understanding the underlying emotions and perspectives. This empathy strengthens connections, as people feel valued and heard. Following up with personalized messages further reinforces these bonds. A thoughtful note or email referencing a specific topic discussed shows that you value the relationship and are invested in its growth. This simple gesture can differentiate you from others and pave the way for continued collaboration and support.

Opportunities for networking abound in various settings, each presenting unique avenues for connection. Industry conferences and seminars provide fertile ground for meeting professionals who share your interests and challenges. These events, often rich with discussions and workshops, offer the chance to engage with thought leaders and peers alike. Professional associations and clubs also serve as valuable networking platforms, bringing together individuals united by common goals and areas of expertise. These groups foster a sense of community and provide ongoing opportunities for collaboration and learning. In today's digital age, social media platforms have become indispensable tools for professional networking. LinkedIn, in particular, offers a space to connect with industry professionals, join relevant groups, and participate in discussions that can enhance your visibility and influence.

Successful networkers exemplify the transformative power of authentic connections. Consider the story of Caroline Pugh, who dedicates a significant portion of her time to strategic networking. Her efforts have resulted in a robust network that supports her career growth and opens doors to new opportunities [†1]. Similarly, Jennifer Justice has leveraged networking to stay top of mind for potential opportunities and to seek valuable advice. Her proactive approach ensures she remains informed and connected within her industry [†1]. These examples illustrate that networking, when approached with intention and sincerity, can significantly enhance career trajectories and expand professional horizons.

	**Interactive Element:** Network Goals Worksheet

This exercise will help you set clear networking objectives, identify opportunities for meaningful connections, and create a follow-up strategy to ensure your networking efforts are intentional and productive.

Step 1: Define Your Networking Objectives

List your top three networking goals for the upcoming year. Be specific about what you want to achieve, whether it's finding a mentor, exploring new career opportunities, or building relationships within your industry.

Template:

Networking Goal:	Why This Goal Is Important
Build relationships with professionals in my field.	Gain insights into industry trends and best practices.
Identify a mentor for career guidance.	Receive support and advice for professional growth.
Expand my network within my organization.	Increase visibility and build collaboration opportunities.

Step 2: Identify Networking Opportunities

List specific events, platforms, or strategies where you can connect with individuals aligned with your goals.

Example Table:

Goal	Event/Platform	Connection Opportunity
Build relationships in my field.	Industry conferences, LinkedIn groups	Attend panels and join group discussions.
Identify a mentor for career guidance.	Company mentoring program	Reach out to experienced leaders.
Expand my network internally.	Departmental meetings, social events	Introduce myself and engage in conversations.

Step 3: Create a Follow-Up Strategy

For each connection you make, plan how you will follow up to strengthen the relationship. Include personalized messages or set up meetings to continue the conversation.

Follow-Up Plan Template:

Contact	How We Connected	Next Steps	Timeline
Jane Doe, industry leader	Met at a conference panel	Send a LinkedIn message and invite for coffee	Within 1 week
John Smith, colleague	Spoke during a team social event	Schedule a one-on-one to discuss collaboration	Within 2 weeks

Step 4: Review and Reflect

Set aside time monthly or quarterly to review your Networking Goals Worksheet. Reflect on your progress and adjust your strategies as needed.

7.2 Finding and Approaching Potential Mentors

Mentorship stands as a cornerstone in professional development, offering a unique blend of guidance and inspiration that fuels both career advancement and personal growth. Defined as a relationship where a more experienced individual imparts wisdom and insight to someone navigating their career path, mentorship transcends mere advice. It is a transformative partnership that empowers you to confront challenges, refine skills, and build confidence in your leadership capabilities.  The value of mentorship lies in the personalized support it provides, tailored to your specific goals and aspirations. Through these relationships, you gain not only practical skills but also the courage to pursue ambitious dreams. Mentors illuminate paths previously unconsidered, offering perspectives that can reshape your approach to both career and personal development.

When seeking a mentor, the selection process must align with both your personal and professional objectives. A mentor should possess complementary skills and experiences that can guide you through the intricacies of your chosen field. Consider individuals whose career paths or leadership styles resonate with your aspirations. Look for mentors who have navigated similar challenges or possess expertise in areas you wish to develop. Equally important is the alignment of values and goals. A mentor who shares your core values will provide advice that is not only strategic but also congruent with your ethical and professional standards. This alignment ensures that the guidance you receive is both relevant and actionable, providing a roadmap that reflects your unique journey and aspirations.

Approaching a potential mentor requires thoughtfulness and preparation. Craft a compelling introduction that succinctly conveys your background, interests, and reasons for seeking mentorship. Highlight specific aspects of their career or achievements that inspire you, demonstrating genuine interest and admiration for their work. Clearly articulate your goals and how their mentorship could facilitate your growth. Expressing genuine interest involves more than admiration; it is about establishing a connection based on shared passions and mutual respect. Offering value in return is crucial in fostering a reciprocal relationship. Consider what you can bring to the table, whether it's fresh perspectives, assistance on projects, or introductions to your own network. This exchange transforms the mentorship into a mutually beneficial partnership, enriching both parties and fostering a dynamic of collaboration and growth.

Stories of successful mentor-mentee pairs illustrate the profound impact of these relationships. Consider a mentee who credits her career breakthrough to the guidance of a seasoned executive in her industry. Through regular mentorship sessions, she gained insights into strategic decision-making and leadership skills, which propelled her into a managerial role. Her mentor, in turn, found satisfaction in witnessing her growth and success, reinforcing the value of giving back. In another field, a renowned scientist attributes his innovative ideas to the mentorship of a senior researcher who encouraged an unconventional approach. Their partnership flourished through shared exploration and intellectual curiosity, resulting in groundbreaking discoveries that advanced their field. Testimonials from mentees emphasize the confidence, clarity, and opportunities gained from mentorship, underscoring its role as a catalyst for career development and personal transformation.

These stories reveal that mentorship is more than a professional relationship; it is a collaboration that fosters mutual growth and learning. As you seek and cultivate mentorships, remember that the process is dynamic and evolving, shaped by mutual respect, shared goals, and a commitment to growth.

7.3 The Mentor-Mentee Relationship: Maximizing Benefits

A thriving mentor-mentee relationship requires a foundation built on mutual respect, clear expectations, and shared goals. Setting clear expectations at the onset of the relationship is crucial. Together, you and your mentor should outline what you hope to achieve, both individually and collectively. This clarity ensures that both parties are aligned and working towards a common objective. It also helps prevent misunderstandings and keeps the relationship-focused and productive. Regular communication is another vital component. Schedule consistent check-ins to discuss progress, challenges, and any evolving goals. These meetings should be a two-way street, allowing both you and your mentor to offer insights and feedback. Such dialogue fosters a dynamic of continuous learning and growth. Feedback is invaluable in this context. It helps identify areas for improvement and provides a platform for celebrating successes. Your mentor's insights can offer a fresh perspective, challenging you to think critically and develop new skills.

To make the most of your mentor-mentee relationship, approach it with preparation and intention. Before each meeting, prepare by reflecting on your recent experiences and identifying specific questions or topics for discussion. This preparation demonstrates your commitment to the relationship and maximizes the time you have with your mentor. Keep your mentor informed of your progress and any significant developments in your career. This transparency not only keeps your mentor engaged but also provides context for the advice they offer. When seeking feedback, be open and receptive. Constructive criticism can be a powerful catalyst for growth, providing the insights needed to refine your approach and enhance your skills. Remember to show appreciation for your mentor's time and guidance. A simple thank you, or acknowledgment of their impact can go a long way in strengthening the relationship. It also reinforces the value you place on their support, encouraging continued investment in your development.

Mentors also stand to gain significantly from these relationships. Engaging with mentees offers mentors fresh perspectives and new ideas.

These interactions can challenge mentors to reconsider their own assumptions and approaches, fostering a cycle of reflection and growth. The satisfaction of giving back and witnessing a mentee's progress and success can be deeply rewarding. It reaffirms the mentor's impact and legacy, offering a sense of fulfillment and purpose. Mentors often find that these relationships reignite their passion for their field, as they are reminded of the excitement and curiosity that initially drew them to their profession. This renewed enthusiasm can translate into revitalized energy and creativity in their work.

Consider the story of Maya and her mentor, Elena, as an example of a mutually beneficial mentor-mentee relationship. Maya, a rising leader in a tech company, sought Elena's guidance to navigate the challenges of her new role. Through regular meetings, they set clear goals for Maya's development, focusing on leadership skills and strategic thinking. Elena's feedback offered Maya new insights, helping her refine her approach and build confidence. In turn, Maya's fresh perspectives and innovative ideas inspired Elena to explore new directions in her own work, fostering a collaborative exchange that benefited both. This partnership not only propelled Maya's career forward, leading to a significant promotion, but also enriched Elena's professional journey, reminding her of the importance of mentorship. Another example is the relationship between a young entrepreneur and her mentor, an experienced business leader. The mentor's guidance helped the entrepreneur navigate the complexities of launching a startup, providing strategic advice and support. This mentorship proved instrumental in the entrepreneur's success, leading to a thriving business and recognition in her industry.

These stories underscore the transformative potential of mentor-mentee relationships. They illustrate how such partnerships can lead to significant personal and professional growth, benefiting both parties in profound and lasting ways. As you navigate your own mentor-mentee relationship, remember that the dynamic is one of collaboration and mutual enrichment, offering opportunities for learning, growth, and success.

7.4 Sponsorship: Taking Mentorship to the Next Level

In the professional landscape, sponsorship represents a pivotal escalation from mentorship, offering a distinct form of support that actively propels your career forward. Sponsors differ from mentors in that they do not simply provide guidance and advice; they advocate for you in influential circles where decisions are made. They use their positions of power to ensure that your name is known, your talents are recognized, and your contributions are valued. This advocacy is particularly crucial in high-stakes environments where visibility can make or break career advancement. Sponsors champion your potential, opening doors to opportunities that might otherwise remain inaccessible. Their influence in these settings can be the catalyst for achieving leadership roles and breaking through glass ceilings. Unlike mentors who focus on personal and professional development, sponsors put their reputation on the line to support your career trajectory, vouching for your capabilities and readiness to take on greater responsibilities.

The benefits of having a sponsor extend beyond mere visibility. Sponsors provide access to critical opportunities that can accelerate your professional growth. They facilitate introductions to key decision-makers, positioning you in places where your skills and talents can be showcased. This visibility is a powerful asset, distinguishing you from peers and positioning you as a leader in your field. Through sponsorship, you gain access to prestigious projects and roles that may not be advertised or available through conventional channels. This insider access accelerates your career progression, allowing you to demonstrate your capabilities in high-profile contexts. Additionally,

sponsors often serve as advocates during promotion discussions, ensuring that your contributions are recognized and rewarded appropriately. This advocacy can be instrumental in navigating organizational hierarchies and securing leadership positions.

Securing a sponsor requires strategic action and a proactive approach. Begin by demonstrating your potential and reliability in your current role. Consistently deliver high-quality work, exceed expectations, and showcase your leadership potential. This establishes your credibility and makes you an attractive candidate for sponsorship. Next, identify potential sponsors within your industry or organization. Look for individuals in influential positions who have the power to advocate on your behalf. Building a relationship with a potential sponsor involves more than just seeking their support; it requires demonstrating how your success aligns with their interests and goals. Engage with them by seeking their advice on projects, sharing your achievements, and expressing your aspirations. By aligning your objectives with theirs, you create a mutually beneficial relationship that encourages their advocacy.

7.5 Engaging with Professional Communities and Groups

In the ever-evolving world of career advancement, engaging with communities and groups offers a wealth of opportunities that extend far beyond traditional networking. Professional communities serve as invaluable ecosystems where knowledge, connections, and support converge to foster development and innovation. These groups provide access to industry insights and emerging trends, equipping you with the information needed to stay ahead in your field. By participating actively in these communities, you gain exposure to diverse perspectives and expertise that broaden your understanding and enhance your skills. This engagement not only bolsters your professional acumen but also positions you as a proactive member of your industry, ready to contribute and thrive.

Active engagement is key to maximizing the benefits of professional communities. Participating in discussions and events allows you to interact with peers and thought leaders, exchanging ideas and learning from their experiences. These interactions provide a platform for collaboration and innovation, sparking new ideas and approaches. Volunteering for leadership roles within these groups further amplifies your involvement, offering opportunities to influence the direction of community initiatives and projects. Taking on such roles not only enhances your leadership skills but also elevates your visibility and credibility within the community. Sharing your expertise through presentations or articles is another powerful way to contribute. By showcasing your knowledge and insights, you establish yourself as a thought leader and resource, attracting others who seek to learn from your experience.

The digital age has transformed how we connect with like-minded professionals, making online communities an integral part of professional engagement. Digital platforms provide vast networks that transcend geographical boundaries, enabling you to connect with individuals from around the globe. Joining relevant LinkedIn groups, for instance, offers a space to engage in discussions, share insights, and expand your professional reach. These groups often host webinars and virtual events, providing convenient opportunities to learn and interact with industry leaders and peers. Engaging in online forums allows you to contribute to ongoing conversations, offering your perspectives and learning from others. These digital interactions foster a sense of community and belonging, connecting you with professionals who share your interests and challenges.

Consider the story of a communications professional who leveraged her involvement in a professional community to drive her career forward. By actively participating in discussions and volunteering for events, she gained exposure to influential leaders and new opportunities. Her commitment to sharing knowledge through articles and presentations further solidified her reputation as a thought leader in her field. As a result, she was invited to speak at prominent industry conferences, expanding her network and influence. Another example is a community leader who used online platforms to connect with professionals worldwide. Through strategic engagement in digital forums and webinars, she built a global network that provided support and collaboration opportunities, leading to significant career advancements.

These examples highlight the transformative impact of community involvement on career growth. By engaging with professional communities, you not only enhance your knowledge and skills but also build a network of support and collaboration that can propel your career to new heights. Whether through active participation, leadership roles, or digital engagement, these communities offer a wealth of opportunities to learn, connect, and succeed. They provide a platform for sharing your insights and expertise, positioning you as a valued member of your professional ecosystem. As you navigate your career, consider how you can leverage these communities to achieve your goals and contribute to the collective advancement of your field.

Interactive Element:

Community Engagement Checklist

This exercise will help you stay organized and intentional in your engagement with professional communities, ensuring you contribute meaningfully and benefit from active participation.

Step 1: List Your Professional Communities

Write down the professional communities, groups, or networks you are a part of (e.g., LinkedIn groups, industry associations, alumni networks).

Template:

Community Name	Purpose/Focus Area	My Role
Women in Leadership Network	Empowering women in leadership	Member
Marketing Professionals Association	Advancing marketing strategies	Contributor

Step 2: Identify Upcoming Opportunities

For each community, research and note upcoming events, discussions, or initiatives you can participate in (e.g., webinars, panel discussions, networking events).

Template:

Community Name	Upcoming Event/Discussion	Date	How I Plan to Participate
Women in Leadership Network	Annual Leadership Conference	June 15	Attend and network
Marketing Professionals Association	Monthly Webinar on Digital Trends	May 20	Present a case study

Step 3: Set Specific Goals for Engagement

Outline your goals for each community. Think about how you can contribute, such as sharing expertise, presenting at events, or volunteering for projects.

Template:

Community Name	Goal	Timeline
Women in Leadership Network	Present a webinar on strategic leadership.	Within 3 months
Marketing Professionals Association	Write an article for their newsletter.	By the end of the quarter

Step 4: Track Your Involvement and Achievements

Use this table to track your participation and reflect on the impact of your engagement.

Template:

Community Name	Activity Completed	Outcome/Impact	Next Steps
Women in Leadership Network	Attended networking session	Built connections with 3 leaders	Follow up with coffee chats.
Marketing Professionals Association	Published an article	Increased visibility in the field	Pitch a second article topic.

Step 5: Reflect and Adjust

At the end of each quarter, review your checklist. Consider:

- *Have I achieved my goals for each community?*
- *What new opportunities can I pursue?*
- *How has my engagement contributed to my professional growth?*

Reflection Prompts:

1. What has been the most rewarding part of engaging with these communities?

2. What skills or insights have I gained through my involvement?

3. How can I deepen my contributions in the future?

7.6 Building a Supportive Network of Peers

Navigating the professional world can be daunting, but a robust network of peers can serve as a lifeline, offering emotional support, collaboration, and shared learning experiences. These networks provide a sense of community and belonging, crucial in environments that can sometimes feel isolating. Emotional support from peers is invaluable, offering encouragement and understanding when challenges arise. This camaraderie fosters an environment of trust and openness, where individuals feel comfortable sharing their struggles and triumphs. Accountability is another significant benefit, as peer networks encourage members to stay focused on their goals and commitments. Knowing that others are invested in your success can motivate you to push through obstacles and strive for excellence.

To cultivate meaningful peer relationships, consider organizing peer support groups. These groups can meet regularly to discuss goals, challenges, and progress, providing a platform for mutual encouragement and accountability. Engaging in collaborative projects with peers also strengthens relationships, as working together towards a common objective fosters cooperation and trust. These projects offer opportunities to learn from one another, share skills, and develop new perspectives that can enhance your professional capabilities. By collaborating with peers, you not only build valuable relationships but also expand your knowledge and expertise, positioning yourself for greater success. Cultivating these connections requires intentionality and effort, but the rewards are well worth it. A strong peer network can be a source of inspiration, support, and growth, providing a foundation for your professional journey.

The role of peer networks in career development cannot be overstated. Peers can offer feedback and insights that are often more relatable and applicable than those from individuals outside your field. They understand the intricacies of your industry and can provide advice and support tailored to your specific context. Sharing industry insights and resources is a key component of peer networks, as members exchange information that can enhance their understanding and keep them informed of emerging trends. Peer mentoring and coaching sessions are another valuable aspect, allowing members to learn from each other's experiences and expertise. These sessions provide opportunities for skill development and personal growth, fostering a culture of continuous learning and improvement.

Successful peer networks have significantly impacted their members' careers, as demonstrated by numerous examples. Consider a group of women in tech who formed a peer network to support one another in navigating a male-dominated industry. Through regular meetings and collaborative projects, they shared valuable insights, resources, and strategies for success. Their collective efforts resulted in several members securing promotions, leading projects, and gaining recognition within their organizations. Testimonials from members highlight the profound impact of this network on their confidence, skills, and career trajectories. Similarly, a peer-led initiative in the healthcare industry brought together professionals from diverse backgrounds to address common challenges and share best practices. This collaboration led to innovative solutions and improvements in patient care, showcasing the transformative potential of peer networks. These stories illustrate that peer networks are not just about support; they are catalysts for growth and success, empowering members to achieve their goals and make meaningful contributions to their fields.

As we conclude this chapter on building strong networks and mentorship, it's clear that these connections play a vital role in career advancement and personal growth. Whether through peer networks, mentorship, or sponsorship, the relationships we cultivate shape our professional journeys and open doors to opportunities that propel us forward. As we move into the next chapter, let us explore the practical strategies and skills needed to navigate the complexities of leadership with confidence and authenticity.

CHAPTER 8: REAL-WORLD INSPIRATION AND APPLICATION

"Every great dream begins with a dreamer. Always remember, you have within you the strength, the patience, and the passion to reach for the stars to change the world."
— Harriet Tubman

8.1 Trailblazing Women

Imagine standing at the edge of a vast ocean, watching waves crash against the shore with unyielding force and rhythm. This image reflects the relentless push and pull of women breaking barriers in leadership, carving out paths where none existed before. Throughout history, countless women have defied norms, challenged the status quo, and achieved remarkable feats in fields where they were often the sole female presence. Their stories are not just tales of personal triumph but are blueprints for the next generation, illustrating resilience, innovation, and the power of vision.

Consider the journey of Mae Jemison, the first African American woman to travel into space. Her path to becoming an astronaut was not just one of academic excellence but also an embodiment of persistent innovation and a relentless pursuit of dreams. Growing up in a time when space exploration was predominantly male-dominated, Jemison not only broke through racial and gender barriers but also inspired countless young girls to reach for the stars. Her career in the STEM field, an area still striving for gender parity, underscores the importance of representation in inspiring future leaders. Jemison's story exemplifies how innovation can be a driving force, not just in personal success but in transforming societal perceptions of what women can achieve.

In the corporate world, stories of pioneering women like the first female CEOs of major corporations serve as beacons of inspiration. These women, often navigating industries that were historically male-dominated, have exemplified qualities of strategic vision and unwavering determination. Their rise to leadership positions was not simply a personal victory but a testament to their ability to innovate and drive change within their organizations. By integrating creativity with strategic thinking, these leaders have not only achieved personal success but have also paved the way for more inclusive and diverse workplaces. Their journeys highlight the importance of lifelong learning and adaptability, traits that are essential in today's rapidly evolving business landscape.

A common thread among these trailblazers is their commitment to lifelong learning. In an ever-changing world, the ability to adapt and learn continuously is a critical skill for any leader. This commitment to learning is not just about acquiring new knowledge but also about applying it to innovate and solve complex problems. Leaders like Indra Nooyi, former CEO of PepsiCo, have demonstrated how a learning mindset can fuel transformational leadership. Her approach to leadership was characterized by empathy, strategic thinking, and an unwavering focus on innovation. Nooyi's leadership style, which prioritized inclusivity and sustainability, left a lasting impact on PepsiCo and the broader business community. Her emphasis on "Performance with Purpose" illustrates how integrating business success with social responsibility can lead to sustainable growth and inspire future generations of leaders.

Indra Nooyi's leadership philosophy offers valuable insights for aspiring leaders. Her approach, which combined empathy with strategic vision, empowered her employees and fostered a culture of collaboration and innovation. By involving employees in decision-making processes, Nooyi demonstrated the power of democratic leadership, where diverse voices contribute to achieving shared goals. Her ability to connect with employees on a personal level fostered trust and loyalty, essential components of effective leadership. Aspiring leaders can draw from Nooyi's example by cultivating an inclusive environment that values diverse perspectives and encourages open communication. Her story underscores the importance of aligning leadership practices with personal values and organizational goals, creating a cohesive and purpose-driven workplace.

Reflecting on the journeys of these trailblazing women, it becomes evident that their success was not rooted in extraordinary circumstances but in their ability to leverage qualities like innovation, resilience, and commitment to learning. As you consider your own leadership path, reflect on the values and traits that resonate with you. Engage in exercises that align your personal values with your leadership goals, ensuring that your journey is not only successful but also authentic and fulfilling. By drawing parallels between your experiences and those of pioneering women leaders, you can identify opportunities for growth and innovation that align with your vision.

8.2 Case Studies in Authentic Leadership

Authentic leadership is more than a leadership style; it is a commitment to lead with integrity, transparency, and a genuine connection to one's values. Consider the case of Howard Schultz, former CEO of Starbucks, whose leadership is a testament to the power of authenticity. Schultz led with a focus on transparency, often sharing his personal journey and the values that shaped his vision for Starbucks. His leadership was marked by bold initiatives, such as offering healthcare benefits to part-time employees, which reflected his belief in the importance of employee welfare. Under his guidance, Starbucks became not just a coffee company but a community-oriented brand that valued its employees and customers alike. Schultz's approach illustrates how leaders who remain true to their values can foster trust and loyalty within their organizations. By prioritizing transparency and integrity, he built a company culture that encouraged collaboration and innovation, leading to sustained success.

The impact of authentic leadership extends beyond individual leaders to influence entire teams and organizations. Authentic leaders foster environments where trust and collaboration thrive, leading to increased employee engagement and satisfaction. Research shows that teams led by authentic leaders exhibit higher levels of trust and are more willing to collaborate, as they feel valued and respected. This collaborative spirit fuels creativity and problem-solving, enabling organizations to navigate challenges with agility and resilience.

One key takeaway is the importance of maintaining authenticity under pressure. Leaders often face situations where external pressures may tempt them to compromise their values or adopt a facade to meet expectations. However, the most effective leaders are those who remain steadfast in their authenticity, even amidst adversity. To maintain authenticity, it is crucial to engage in regular reflection and self-assessment. By taking the time to evaluate personal values and how they align with actions, leaders can ensure that their decisions are consistent with their core beliefs. Another strategy is to cultivate a support network of mentors and peers who can provide guidance and hold leaders accountable to their values. This network serves as a sounding board for navigating complex challenges while staying true to one's principles.

Encouraging the application of authentic leadership principles in your own leadership style can lead to transformative outcomes. Start by engaging in reflection exercises that explore your personal authenticity. Consider the values that are most important to you and how they influence your leadership approach. Reflect on past situations where you may have acted inconsistently with your values and identify steps to realign your actions with your beliefs. These exercises help build self-awareness and establish a strong foundation for authentic leadership.

Additionally, develop an action plan that outlines specific ways to incorporate authenticity into your daily leadership practices. This plan might include setting aside time for open dialogue with your team, making decisions that reflect your values, and modeling transparency in your interactions. By consciously integrating authenticity into your leadership style, you create an environment where trust, collaboration, and innovation can flourish.

8.3 The Power of Resilience in Leadership Journeys

In leadership, resilience stands as a cornerstone of success, embodying the ability to withstand adversity and emerge stronger. It is the inner fortitude that enables leaders to navigate setbacks and challenges, transforming obstacles into opportunities for growth. Consider a leader in the public sector who faced intense scrutiny and criticism during a crisis. Rather than succumbing to pressure, she demonstrated resilience by maintaining her composure and focusing on solutions, ultimately restoring trust and credibility in her leadership. Her journey exemplifies how resilience not only helps leaders endure challenges but also fosters innovation and growth, turning adversity into a catalyst for positive change.

The pathway to resilience begins with a shift in mindset, viewing failures not as endpoints but as stepping stones to greater achievements. Embracing this perspective allows leaders to approach challenges with a sense of opportunity rather than defeat. For instance, a tech entrepreneur who experienced multiple startup failures before achieving success illustrates this mindset. Each setback taught her valuable lessons, which she leveraged to refine her approach and ultimately build a groundbreaking company. By adopting a growth-oriented mindset, she transformed past failures into a foundation for future success, demonstrating that resilience often leads to innovation and breakthroughs.

Building supportive networks is another critical strategy for fostering resilience. Just as a tree draws strength from its roots, leaders draw resilience from a network of supportive peers, mentors, and colleagues. These networks provide not only emotional support but also practical advice and diverse perspectives that can guide leaders through difficult times. A healthcare executive who navigated a challenging merger credits her resilience to the strong network of mentors and peers who offered guidance and encouragement throughout the process. This support network bolstered her confidence and provided the insights needed to make informed decisions, reinforcing the importance of building and nurturing professional relationships.

Stories of leaders who exemplify resilience abound, offering inspiration and guidance for those seeking to cultivate this vital trait. One such leader is a renowned scientist who faced numerous rejections before her groundbreaking research was recognized. Her unwavering determination and resilience enabled her to persevere through countless setbacks, ultimately resulting in a discovery that revolutionized her field. Her story serves as a testament to the power of resilience in overcoming obstacles and achieving remarkable success.

To cultivate resilience, it's essential to adopt practices that reinforce a resilient mindset and lifestyle. Journaling can be a powerful tool for reflection and self-discovery, allowing leaders to process their experiences and emotions. By regularly journaling about challenges faced and lessons learned, leaders can gain clarity and develop a deeper understanding of their resilience journey. Additionally, setting specific resilience-building goals can help leaders focus their efforts on strengthening this vital trait. These goals might include developing new skills, seeking feedback, or engaging in activities that promote mental and emotional well-being.

Engaging in regular reflection through journaling not only enhances self-awareness but also provides a written record of growth and progress. This practice encourages leaders to acknowledge their resilience in the face of challenges, providing a source of motivation and confidence during difficult times. By consistently setting and working toward resilience-building goals, leaders can create a proactive approach to personal and professional development, ensuring they are prepared to navigate future challenges with strength and determination.

8.4 Your Leadership Legacy: Inspiring Future Generations

Consider for a moment the concept of legacy—a leadership legacy, in particular. This isn't merely about the accolades and achievements that one accumulates over a career. Rather, it's about the enduring impact you leave on your organization, your community, and the people whose lives you've touched. A leadership legacy is composed of the values you've imparted, the culture you've fostered, and the change you've inspired. It is a testament to the principles that guided your decisions and the vision that fueled your efforts. This legacy is what remains long after you've moved on, influencing future leaders and setting a precedent for those who follow.

The importance of consciously shaping your legacy cannot be overstated. As leaders, we often focus on immediate goals and challenges, but the broader narrative of our leadership is what will ultimately define us. Intentional legacy building involves aligning daily actions with long-term goals, ensuring that each decision contributes to the bigger picture you wish to create. Leaders like Ruth Bader Ginsburg, whose legacy extends beyond her legal achievements to encompass her unwavering commitment to equality and justice, exemplify the power of a thoughtfully constructed legacy. Her work transformed the landscape of gender rights, and her legacy continues to inspire those who advocate for equality today. By consciously shaping your legacy, you ensure that your contributions extend beyond your tenure, influencing future generations and promoting lasting change.

To begin building your leadership legacy, start by identifying your core values and the contributions you wish to make. Reflect on what drives you and what you hope to achieve through your leadership. These values should serve as the foundation of your legacy, guiding your actions and decisions. Engaging in mentorship and community service can also be valuable components of your legacy. By mentoring others, you pass on your knowledge and experience, empowering the next generation of leaders. Community service allows you to contribute to the greater good, reinforcing the values you hold dear and setting an example for others to follow. These activities not only enhance your legacy but also enrich your leadership experience, providing new perspectives and opportunities for growth.

As you contemplate the legacy you wish to leave, take time to envision the impact you want to have. Reflection exercises can be invaluable in this process, helping you articulate your aspirations and identify the steps needed to achieve them. Consider creating a personal legacy statement that encapsulates your vision and the principles you wish to uphold. This statement serves as a guiding beacon, reminding you of your long-term goals and the legacy you are building. It can be as simple or as detailed as you wish, but it should resonate with your core beliefs and inspire you to act with purpose and intention. By crafting a clear and compelling legacy statement, you create a framework for your leadership that aligns your daily actions with your overarching vision, ensuring that each step you take contributes to the legacy you wish to leave behind.

Reflection Exercise:

Legacy Planning Worksheet

Take a moment to reflect on the legacy you want to create as a leader. Use this exercise to clarify your values, actions, and long-term impact.

Step 1: Your Core Values

Write down three values that are central to your leadership style. Examples: Integrity, empathy, innovation, collaboration, or resilience.

1.

2.

3.

Step 2: Identify Your Contributions

List three ways you want to contribute through your leadership:

- In your words (e.g., inspiring others, advocating for equality).
- In your actions (e.g., creating opportunities, leading by example).

Step 3: Align Your Practices

Reflect on your current leadership practices:

- How do they align with the values and contributions you've identified?

- Are there any gaps or areas for improvement?

What I'm doing well:

What I need to improve:

Step 4: Plan for Growth and Impact

Think about how you can further your legacy through mentorship, community involvement, or advocacy.

- Who can you mentor or guide?

- What causes or initiatives can you support to extend your impact?

Step 5: Create Your Leadership Legacy Statement

Combine your reflections into a short statement summarizing the legacy you want to leave.

Example: "I want to be remembered as a leader who inspired innovation, empowered others to reach their potential, and created opportunities for positive change."

Your Leadership Legacy Statement:

Conclusion

As you reach the culmination of this journey through "The Power of Women in Leadership," it is essential to revisit the key themes and strategies that have been woven throughout the text. This book has served as a comprehensive guide, exploring the multifaceted aspects of leadership specific to women. It has addressed the critical importance of building confidence, embracing authentic leadership styles, navigating the intricacies of workplace dynamics, and achieving a harmonious work-life balance. Furthermore, it has offered strategies for advancing your career authentically, overcoming systemic barriers, and fostering robust networks and mentorships. Through real-world examples and narratives, the book has illustrated the profound impact women can have when they lead with authenticity and courage.

The core takeaways from this book are both practical and empowering. Building confidence requires understanding and leveraging your unique strengths. Embracing vulnerability not as a weakness but as a strength fosters deeper connections and trust. Overcoming imposter syndrome with cognitive strategies can liberate you from self-doubt and open new vistas of opportunity. Authentic leadership, characterized by integrity and transparency, enhances personal growth and catalyzes organizational success. As you advance in your career, these lessons will serve as a compass, guiding you toward a leadership style that is both effective and true to your values.

Now, as you stand on the precipice of change and growth, the transformative potential of these lessons beckons. Implement the strategies and insights gleaned from this book in your leadership journey. Unlock the opportunities to empower yourself and those around you. Remember that each step you take toward authentic leadership can inspire and elevate others. Your journey is not solitary; it is part of a larger movement that champions the unique contributions of women in leadership.

I urge you to take proactive steps toward your leadership goals. Share your journey with others and create networks of support and collaboration. Advocate for systemic changes within your workplace to foster an environment where diversity and inclusion thrive. Your voice and actions can pave the way for future generations of women leaders. Engage with additional resources that can further enhance your growth. Explore recommended readings, participate in coaching programs, and join online communities where you can connect with like-minded individuals and continue your personal and professional development.

I am deeply grateful for your engagement with this book. Your commitment to harnessing your leadership potential is inspiring. As you move forward, know that you are not alone in this endeavor. You are part of a vibrant community of women leaders who are redefining what it means to lead with confidence and authenticity.

I believe in every woman's potential to lead boldly and authentically, and I hope this book catalyzes your growth and success.

Lead with conviction and authenticity. Trust in your ability to effect meaningful change. Together, we can create a future where women leaders thrive and inspire others to do the same. Your journey is just beginning, and the possibilities are limitless.

Make a Difference with Your Review!

Empower Women, One Review at a Time

Your voice matters. *The Power of Women in Leadership* is more than a book—it's a movement. By sharing your thoughts, you help others gain the confidence, insights, and tools to lead boldly.

A few words or a heartfelt reflection can make a difference. **Your review** encourages more women to unlock their leadership journey and amplifies the message of empowerment.

Join the conversation. Share your perspective and be part of the change.

Thank you for your support!

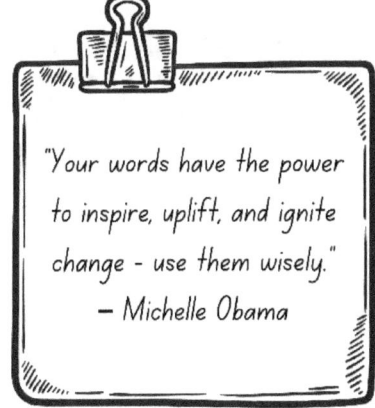

"Your words have the power to inspire, uplift, and ignite change - use them wisely."
— Michelle Obama

REFERENCES

1. [†1] Zenger Folkman. (n.d.). *The Confidence Gap in Men and Women: How to Overcome It*. Retrieved from https://zengerfolkman.com/articles/the-confidence-gap-in-men-and-women-how-to-overcome-it/

2. Brown, B. (n.d.). *Dare to Lead Hub*. Retrieved from https://brenebrown.com/hubs/dare-to-lead/

3. Intentional Outcomes. (n.d.). *Navigating the Maze with Cognitive Behavioral Therapy*. Retrieved from https://intentionaloutcomes.com/decoding-impostor-syndrome-navigating-the-maze-with-cognitive-behavioral-therapy/

4. Dame Leadership. (n.d.). *How a Growth Mindset Shapes Leadership Skills*. Retrieved from https://www.dameleadership.com/research-and-insights/how-a-growth-mindset-shapes-leadership-skills/

5. Coach Padraig. (n.d.). *Women in Leadership: Diversity in Leadership Styles*. Medium. Retrieved from https://medium.com/@coachpadraig/women-in-leadership-diversity-in-leadership-styles-2eb5fb92620e

6. Harvard Business School. (n.d.). *Emotional Intelligence in Leadership: Why It's Important*. Retrieved from https://online.hbs.edu/blog/post/emotional-intelligence-in-leadership

7. Arruda, W. (2024, October 2). *How Women Can Use Personal Branding to Accelerate Career Success*. Forbes. Retrieved from https://www.forbes.com/sites/williamarruda/2024/10/02/how-women-use-personal-branding-for-career-success/

8. Vocare Leadership. (n.d.). *The Art of Leadership: Balancing Assertiveness and Empowerment*. Retrieved from https://www.vocareleadership.com/blog/the-art-of-leadership-balancing-assertiveness-and-empowerment

9. Harvard Business Review. (2012, June). *Strategic Alliances Can Make or Break Female Leaders*. Retrieved from https://hbr.org/2012/06/strategic-alliances-can-make-o

10. Harvard Business Review. (2022, January). *How Women Can Get Comfortable "Playing Politics" at Work*. Retrieved from https://hbr.org/2022/01/how-women-can-get-comfortable-playing-politics-at-work

11. Satyn Magazine. (n.d.). *Mastering Communication in a Male-Dominated World*. Retrieved from https://satynmag.com/mastering-communication-in-a-male-dominated-world/

12. PSCI. (n.d.). *Handling Feedback and Criticism: Turning Challenges into Career Growth*. Retrieved from https://www.psci.com/handling-feedback-and-criticism-turning-challenges-into-career-growth/

13. Loflin, J. (n.d.). *How Setting Healthy Boundaries Makes You a Stronger Leader*. Retrieved from https://jonesloflin.com/jonesloflinblog/leadership-setting-healthy-boundaries/

14. Forbes Coaches Council. (2023, October 5). *Mastering the Art of Delegation for Female Leaders*. Forbes. Retrieved from https://www.forbes.com/councils/forbescoachescouncil/2023/10/05/mastering-the-art-of-delegation-for-female-leaders/

15. Mayo Clinic. (n.d.). *Mindfulness Exercises*. Retrieved from https://www.mayoclinic.org/healthy-lifestyle/consumer-health/in-depth/mindfulness-exercises/art-20046356

16. Building Champions. (n.d.). *6 Steps for Women Leaders to Find Work-Life Balance*. Retrieved from https://www.buildingchampions.com/blog/6-steps-for-women-leaders-to-find-work-life-balance

17. Ellevate. (2019, December 23). *Secrets to Confidence for Every Woman Leader*. Forbes. Retrieved from https://www.forbes.com/sites/ellevate/2019/12/23/secrets-to-confidence-for-every-woman-leader/

18. AWL Online. (n.d.). *Balancing the Work-Life Scales as a Female Leader*. Retrieved from https://awlonline.co.uk/balancing-the-scales-work-life-harmony-for-women-leaders/

19. Think with Google. (n.d.). *Women in the Workplace: 5 Women's Career Stories*. Retrieved from https://www.thinkwithgoogle.com/future-of-marketing/management-and-culture/women-in-the-workplace/

20. The Growth Faculty. (n.d.). *8 Inspirational Female Leaders Who Broke the Glass Ceiling*. Retrieved from https://thegrowthfaculty.com/articles/inspirationalfemaleleaders

21. American Association of University Women (AAUW). (n.d.). *Barriers & Bias: The Status of Women in Leadership*. Retrieved from https://www.aauw.org/resources/research/barrier-bias/

22. AIHR. (2025). *13 Tried-and-Tested DEI Initiatives to Implement [In 2025]*. Retrieved from https://www.aihr.com/blog/dei-initiatives/

23. University of Missouri Business School. (n.d.). *Opportunities for Advancement: Gender Bias in the Workplace*. Retrieved from https://business.missouri.edu/about/news/opportunities-advancement-gender-bias-workplace

24. WeQual. (n.d.). *The Importance of Allyship in the Workplace*. Retrieved from https://wequal.com/insight/importance-of-allyship-in-the-workplace/

25. Marcus, B. (2018, April 10). *How Successful Women Network for Their Career and Business*. Forbes. Retrieved from https://www.forbes.com/sites/bonniemarcus/2018/04/10/how-successful-women-network-for-their-career-and-business/

26. Mentoring Complete. (n.d.). *Effective Women Mentorship Strategies: Empower & Inspire*. Retrieved from https://www.mentoringcomplete.com/women-mentorship-strategies/

27. Chronus. (n.d.). *What is a Mentor vs a Sponsor and Why Incorporate Both?*. Retrieved from https://chronus.com/blog/sponsorship-vs-mentorship-why-not-both/

28. The Comms Avenue. (n.d.). *How to Leverage Professional Communities for Career Growth*. Retrieved from https://thecommsavenue.com/how-to-leverage-professional-communities-for-career-growth/

29. Obama White House Archives. (n.d.). *The Untold History of Women in Science and Technology*. Retrieved from https://obamawhitehouse.archives.gov/women-in-stem

30. Strategy Punk. (n.d.). *Indra Nooyi's Leadership Style: Key Insights and Impact*. Retrieved from https://www.strategypunk.com/indra-nooyis-leadership-style-key-insights-and-impact/

31. Center for Creative Leadership. (n.d.). *Authentic Leadership: What It Is, Why It Matters*. Retrieved from https://www.ccl.org/articles/leading-effectively-articles/authenticity-1-idea-3-facts-5-tips/

32. Center for Creative Leadership. (n.d.). *8 Practices for More Resilient Leadership*. Retrieved from https://www.ccl.org/articles/leading-effectively-articles/8-steps-help-become-resilient/

www.ingramcontent.com/pod-product-compliance
Lightning Source LLC
LaVergne TN
LVHW012021060526
838201LV00061B/4396